FROM THE WARD TO THE WHITE HOUSE

ALSO BY GEORGE E. REEDY

The Twilight of the Presidency: Johnson to Reagan
The U.S. Senate: Paralysis or Search for Consensus?
Lyndon B. Johnson: A Memoir
The Presidency in Flux
The Twilight of the Presidency
Who Will Do Our Fighting for Us?

FROM *the* WARD *to the* WHITE HOUSE

♣

The Irish in American Politics

GEORGE E. REEDY

Charles Scribner's Sons   *New York*

Collier Macmillan Canada   *Toronto*

Maxwell Macmillan International
New York   Oxford   Singapore   Sydney

Copyright © 1991 by George E. Reedy

Charles Scribner's Sons
Macmillan Publishing Company
866 Third Avenue, New York, NY 10022

Collier Macmillan Canada, Inc.
1200 Eglinton Avenue East, Suite 200
Don Mills, Ontario M3C 3N1

Library of Congress Cataloging-in-Publication Data
Reedy, George E.————.
From the ward to the White House : the Irish in American politics / George E. Reedy.
p. cm.
Includes bibliographical references and index.
ISBN 0-684-18977-1
1. Irish Americans—Politics and government. I. Title.
E184.I6R44 1991
973'.049162—dc20   90-43266   CIP

10 9 8 7 6 5 4 3 2 1

Printed in the United States of America

This book is dedicated to three Reedys—

*my Great-Grandfather Michael; my Grandfather William;
and my Father George.*

They were so preoccupied fighting for survival,
with few resources other than wit and guts,
that they had no time to discover their place
in a major current of America's historic stream.

♣

CONTENTS

Acknowledgments ix

1 Where It Began *1*

2 The Forging of a Nation *14*

3 A Square Meal *23*

4 The Promised Land *33*

5 The Lumpenproletariat *43*

6 The As and Bs of the Irish Machines *57*

7 The Nuts and Bolts *73*

8 The Spreading Power *85*

9 The Threshold of the National Stage *97*

10 Purgation *109*

Contents

11   The Roaring Twenties   *121*

12   A Bridge Too Far   *133*

13   From Paddy to Patrick   *143*

14   The Boss of Bosses   *155*

15   The Afterglow   *169*

16   Judgment Day   *181*

Appendix:
Why the Ward Boss Rules   JANE ADDAMS   191

Bibliography   199

Index   205

ACKNOWLEDGMENTS

THERE ARE MANY PEOPLE AND ORGANIZATIONS TO WHOM I MUST acknowledge deep indebtedness in writing this book. First, I cite two indefatigable research assistants—Chris Day, who is Irish, and Michael Houston, who is Irish-American. Both took a personal interest in the topic and did work far beyond the strict bounds of duty.

Drs. Thomas E. Hachey, of Marquette University, and Lawrence McCaffrey, of Loyola University in Chicago, the eminent Irish historians, reviewed portions of the manuscript and set me straight on important points. Historical errors, if any are found, mean that I produced some sections of the book after they looked at it.

The staffs of the John F. Kennedy, Harry S Truman and Boston Public libraries were very helpful in locating and reproducing for me the pictures and cartoons that give extra life to what I have written and my thanks are due to them as well as to the librarians of the Chicago Tribune. Finally, I am grateful to Charles P. Pierce, a former student, and Steve Repati, graduate records clerk in Marquette's College of Communication, for searching out both pictures and sources and to Bea Bourgeois, who typed the manuscript.

Chapter 1

♣

WHERE IT BEGAN

THIS IS A BOOK THAT MUST BE PUT IN CONTEXT, AND A WORD OR two of explanation is absolutely essential. I am not a professional historian or a cultural anthropologist, and my degree in sociology does not include a certificate qualifying me for sweeping judgments on social forces. My friends may well wonder why I am doing a work that requires me to spend so much time reaching back into a past that exists today only in the memory of people my age and in little-read books deploring the corruption of the Irish political machines, which ruled our big cities in the first quarter of this century. The last machine with real power died with Mayor Daley of Chicago, and he was something of an anachronism. Had there been a "last man's" club of urban bosses, he would have taken the prize.

The answer to why I am doing this can be divided into two parts. The first is that my lifetime has been spent either in active participation in politics or in journalism with assignments close to politics. The second is that I am Irish by descent on both sides of my family (my mother was a Mulvaney), and I have a desire to trace my roots. These are not really two separate reasons, since they mesh with each other. Politics, despite all the quantitative studies of the behavioral sciences, remains a matter of social personality. And when it comes to the Irish character, it found its expression here in the United States in politics, because there was no other vehicle that offered our Potato Famine immigrants passage out of the slums.

As a child, my knowledge of Irish history and literature was virtually nil. We lived on the lower East Side of Chicago—an area that in those days was almost entirely Gaelic. My father had only a grammar school education, which he had received on the Upper

[3]

Peninsula of Michigan where he was a member of a family of lumberjacks. Ossian, Fionn Mac Cumhail, Wolfe Tone, Dean Swift, Lady Gregory, Sean O'Casey, and William Butler Yeats meant nothing to him. He did know about Sean Russell, chief of staff of the Irish Republican Army, who toured the United States every year seeking contributions. Otherwise, his roster of prominent Irishmen bore such names as Mike Egan, assistant chief of detectives, Dan Collins, captain of the East Chicago Avenue police station, Dion (Little Diony) O'Banion, the city's top Celtic gunslinger, and Father Pat Malloy, who was much more influential in maintaining law and order in the district than the mayor, the City Council, the district attorney, and the Police Department combined.

There were no leprechauns or wandering minstrel boys on the East Side, and while shillelaghs were in frequent use, no one knew the word. They were called billies or billie clubs, and none of them had been brought from Ireland by anybody's father. What *had* been brought from Ireland was a burning hatred of anything that sounded English. There was a ferocity behind this that had to be seen at close hand to be credited. The Irish could look at Italians, Poles, and even blacks with an air of tolerance that must have been infuriating to the recipients of such patronizing attention. But anyone who substituted a *y* for the *i* in Smith and added an *e* to the end of the name had better be accompanied by fearless bodyguards when traveling through the area. The feeling was kept alive by Irish schoolteachers, who were predominant in the Chicago Public School system of the day. My childhood memories are of a long succession of teachers named O'Malley, Collins, O'Rourke, and Kelly.

There was one in particular named Hayes. (I never did learn her first name; all the pupils referred to her as Old Lady Hayes.) Calling the roll on the first day of the term, she came to me and said: "Reedy! Reedy! Are your folks from County Clare?" I didn't have the faintest idea, but some ancestral instinct of survival told me that the answer had better be affirmative, and I said yes. (I learned when I went home that I was right.) After that, I could

[4]

hand in a blank sheet of paper, and it would come back marked A+ as long as my name was on it. It turned out to be quite a year. At least twice a week she told us about her cousin who, she said, had had his fingernails pulled out by the Black and Tans during the "troubles" and we were instructed that the proper term for England was Perfidious Albion, which was to be pronounced as though it were one word. She was convinced that "King George" had rewritten our textbooks and eliminated the names of Irish-American Revolutionary War heroes. I was left with an impression that there was a room in Buckingham Palace where broad-bottomed Dukes repaired every day to examine the books offered to Chicago schoolchildren. Strangely, I could find no evidence to validate this concept when I actually went to Great Britain many years later.

Aside from Anglophobia, being Irish meant that you helped people with Irish names and expected people with Irish names to help you. There was very little ritual connected with the status. On St. Patrick's Day, everyone went to Mass and wore a white carnation, delicately tinted with green. Afterward, of course, many libations would be poured of rotgut booze and needled beer (this was during Prohibition), but that didn't really set it apart from any other day. The people around me were largely from Potato Famine ancestry, and their forebears had not brought the rich traditions of Erin to the New World because they hadn't had them in the Old World either. They were too busy trying to grub out a living in the face of excruciating hardships.

My father was more exaggeratedly Irish than most of our neighbors. This was probably because he was only half Irish. His mother was Scots—something I did not learn until my teens when my own mother let the fact slip, and he had to make a reluctant confession. He and his mother had not been able to get along, and my father left home when he was only twelve. He spent a few years in Chicago as part of a group of young Irish lads supervised by Father Malloy and then joined the cavalry (lying about his age). At fifteen, he was a one-legged veteran of the fighting with Pancho Villa on the Mexican border. He had tried to burn the knowledge

[5]

of his Scots ancestors out of his mind, and I sometimes think that he married my mother because her name was Mulvaney—then regarded as the ultimate Irish name because of the Kipling stories. Actually, she was Protestant, although not Orange. He never cleared up for me the mystery of why his father—an Irish Catholic—had married a Scotswoman from a Covenanter's family.

In addition to his exaggerated sense of his Irishness, however, my father had other qualities. He was daring and quick-witted and finally got us out of the slums. He had discovered journalism—a craft at which he was very good despite his lack of education. The top news stories of the time involved the Prohibition gangs, who had transformed criminality into big business, and Dad knew most of the Irish gangsters. The record should show that he was honest and never tempted to join them. But they had been—with him—part of the group that had been held together when they were teenagers by Father Malloy. The result was that he had access to news from circles that could not be penetrated by journalists with more extensive educational endowments. In addition, it was an era when most reporters were not expected to do any writing. The facts they adduced were turned over to rewrite men, who whipped them into shape for printing. Almost everything in the *Chicago Tribune*, my father's employer, was produced by two men—"Doc" Dwyre and Walter Fitzmaurice. All that was expected of a beat man was an ability to sort out facts from fiction and, if a little imagination intruded into the process, to coat pseudo-facts with a libel-proof casing similar to the buffering of aspirin.

My later studies convinced me that the history of the American Irish should be divided into four stages. At first, they were looked upon as a menace—drunken hoodlums and barroom brawlers, who came to the United States to effectuate a Papist Plot to bring the nation under the rule of Rome. These were the times that produced very crude books, obviously frauds, such as *The Confessions of a Nun*, the highly suspect trials of the so-called Molly Maguires in the Pennsylvania coal fields, and the Know-Nothing movement, whose major political platform was to expel all the Irish and ban all further Irish immigration.

The Papist Plot theory was too ridiculous to retain credence as the Irish became better known to the Americans already here. The exiles from the Potato Famine managed to work their way into some main channels of American life. The movement began through some process, which is still a mystery, resulting in the takeover of big city police and fire departments. Police, in those days, walked beats and were familiar characters in the neighborhoods they protected. It was possible to think of Clancy as a bomb tosser when he lived in slums where no WASP dared tread. But when he became a big cop with a warm smile who helped your kids cross a street, it was impossible to see him as a devious agent of a foreign pontiff seeking to undermine the foundations of society. Of course, he was still looked upon as "different" and not quite on the same intellectual level as the people who came here earlier. So Clancy became a comic figure—a glib, somewhat irresponsible clown who had little talent other than skill at fisticuffs and at judging pot-still whiskey. The Pat and Mike jokes became the focus for humor in America. Some of them were genuinely funny, but most of them had the same qualities as the Izzy and Jakey gags of a later era and the Polish jokes of modern times.

The third division of American-Irish history covers the period which respectability was gained. This had its origins in a number of developments. Control of the police and the firefighters gave the Irish something to trade—friendly contact with large numbers of citizens who could be made into well-wishers by an "understanding" enforcement of the laws. This, in turn, led to the capture of aldermanic posts, city jobs, and ultimately City Hall itself. Furthermore, professional boxing gave the Celtic population a type of prestige that was *not* patronizing. People could laugh with condescension at jokes about Pat and Mike. But any type of humor involving John L. Sullivan, the Boston Strong Boy, or Gentleman Jim Corbett was bound to be admiring, rather than patronizing. Furthermore, baseball, which was rapidly becoming *the* American sport, boasted Mike Kelly and other Irishmen; at least half of the early Hall of Famers were Irishmen. To round things off, intellectual standing was achieved first through lawyers turned out by Catholic universities such as Fordham, Marquette, and Notre Dame, and later by Irish writers such as Farrell and Greeley.

The final stage was epitomized by the election of John Fitzgerald Kennedy as President of the United States. In a very real sense, that ended the Irish as an identifiable element of the population. We had "passed," so to speak. Of course, the Irish rituals became more pronounced as the reality of the Irish community faded into memory. St. Patrick's Day became a ceremony in which all kinds of people participated, regardless of ancestry. The American Conference on Irish Studies was formed, largely as a device to open new academic fields for aspiring college professors. Irish publications circulate throughout the United States. But what is left of Irish community is centered in a few small areas of Chicago, Boston, and New York, and the people in those areas are dwindling. The reality is summed up in my two sons, who have no concept of Gaelic descent whatsoever. Their attitude was expressed by one of them when he was reading a book I wrote on Selective Service, which I opened by describing the lives of my father and two of my mother's cousins when they were young. They all joined the army voluntarily, because even at the risk of their lives, it was still brighter than anything they could find at home. When I asked my younger son what he thought about the Foreword to the book, he replied: "Oh! You mean the part about *your* family!" He could not conceive of these people being *his* family, because they had nothing to do with his world.

My childhood was spent in one of the early stages of the third period. Being Irish was still something of a joke, and the only Irish writers who were close to a national reputation were Finley Peter Dunne and Frank Ward O'Malley, who wrote what was regarded as a humorous column in the New York *Sun* and produced a book called *The Swiss Family O'Malley*, which recounted his travels throughout Europe. By that time, however, the Irish boxers had become established legends, and when Mike McTige fought

[8]

Mickey Walker for the Light Heavyweight championship of the world on St. Patrick's Day, the Chicago Coliseum was loaded with very proud Micks. What was much more important to Chicago was that something else was becoming loaded with Micks—the district attorney's office. And what was even more important to me was that we had moved out of the "near East Side" to a recently constructed apartment building in an area which was *not* restricted to White Protestants only. It was open to Irish and other Catholics, Jews, and even a few Asians (chiefly Chinese who ran restaurants). Only blacks were excluded.

In this non-Irish area, my concept of Irishness was broadened. There were two reasons for this development. The first was friendly contact on a daily basis with Russian and Polish Jews, Italians from Naples and Sicily, and Swedes. Curiosity about their lives stimulated curiosity about my own background, something I had taken for granted up to that time. The second development that piqued my curiosity was a remarkable high school teacher named Plunkett, who opened to me the universe of classic literature. This meant both American and British authors primarily. But it also included Lady Gregory, John Millington Synge, William Butler Yeats, and George Bernard Shaw. Through them, I discovered there was much more to the Irish heritage than the ability to draw up mutual survival pacts among Reedy, Clancy, Kelly, Mulvaney, Muldoon, and the other descendants of the Wild Geese. That left me wondering what I had really inherited from my ancestry.

It did not take me long to learn that very little information was available in this country. All I really knew was that my Great Grandfather Michael (he spelled the last name Reidy) had married a girl named Margaret King and emigrated from County Clare to the United States sometime during the worst years of the Potato Famine. He had a son named William James, who changed the spelling of the last name to its present form. But the Reedys were a scattered family whose young men had a tradition of leaving home early and never coming back. Stability was not a predominant characteristic, and this meant that none of the individual members had the normal clan information. Years later, when I actually got to Ireland, I found the situation even messier. County Clare was one of the hardest hit of the famine counties, and records were in chaos. I found cemeteries with Reidy tombstones and came across a few people whose features were so close to those of my father that there simply had to be a relationship. But I was unable to trace anyone who could have been my great grandfather, and the best I could do was to obtain some historical information— for example, that the Reidys resulted from Viking raids up the River Shannon and that the name in Gaelic was spelled Riadha (after the Viking Rudh, which meant "red-headed"). There was also a story that the Reidys were once Kings of Connaught, but I had already developed a feeling of skepticism toward tales of the Irish kings and contented myself with thanking my informant—a librarian at Trinity College in Dublin.

Obviously, I could not trace my specific bloodlines without a major search, which was beyond my means. So I settled for trying to trace my cultural heritage. Even here, there were problems. First, Ireland was a country that had been settled in successive waves by the Sons of the Mil (whoever they were), Saxons, Vikings, Normans, and possibly some Spanish—all of whom had been absorbed into a common culture. Beyond that, however, there were several types that developed naturally. There were the Peat Bog Irish (I suspect that was me), the flannel-mouth Irish (not a term used in Ireland but still descriptive), the Anglo-Irish, and the Tinkers (often itinerants). In addition, much of what is known about Irish history consists of unwritten stories passed down from generation to generation of *seanachies*, wandering storytellers who traded an evening's entertainment for bed and board. Early in this century, Lady Gregory financed a project to put on paper the tales of the few who still existed at the time. Whenever their historical allusions could be checked, they turned out to be fairly close to the records. But the problem of determining their historicity is akin to that of the archaeologists who have sought to determine the authenticity of the Iliad—which was transmitted to others orally for a few centuries before it was reduced to writing.

The difficulties did not stop me from learning what I could.

But real light did not shine upon my studies until I began to ponder a seemingly unrelated problem that was connected to my work as a reporter. It was the wide divergence between the blueprints of our government as laid down by the Founding Fathers and the actual workings of our system in the twentieth century. The basic framework of the Constitution remained intact and had stood up well despite some heavy strains. But the actual exercise of gaining and exercising power in the twentieth century would have bewildered the men who drafted our basic charter.

The authors of the Constitution had thought of a government by gentlemen—one in which an educated elite would arrive, through discussion, at the most rational solution available for our problems. They had also expressed horror at the thought that political parties (which they termed "factions") might intrude on the orderly operations of our government. They were rather careful to restrict the franchise to gentlemen—an Electoral College to select Presidents and the appointment of Senators by state legislators, rather than by direct election. The only institution that afforded the average citizen an opportunity to exert pressure on the government directly was the House of Representatives.

At the time the Constitution was produced, such a world could be envisioned. The population was white, Anglo-Saxon, Protestant—except for a few people of Dutch and French descent, not enough to make trouble. The blacks, of course, were completely out of it, even though slavery—or at least the slave trade—had already become an issue that had to be compromised before agreement could be obtained at the Constitutional Convention. There were basically only two vital elements—the commercial shipping areas of the North and the agricultural areas of the South. Whatever they could agree upon they could do.

This situation did not last very long. Pioneers striking into the Appalachian region were too far away to be controlled by the traders and large-scale planters, and the lives they were leading tended to foster independence. It was only a matter of time until they began to unite into political parties led by men like Andrew Jackson. Other changes were fostered by the growth of industry and improved transportation. But one of the sources of the change was the unexpected influx of the Potato Famine Irish. There was no way that the Founding Fathers could have anticipated this development or what it would do to national politics.

The Irish were the first heavy migration of non-WASP settlers who seized upon politics as a means of making a living. They had been preceded by the Scots, who were also Celtic, but Celts whose fathers or grandfathers had taken the Oath of Culloden, and they were not in a mood to make troublesome enclaves and gangster-ridden slums in America's larger cities. The Irish were in a mood to make a lot of such trouble, and they were in desperate search of a way of making a living. They did not have the education to go into business at any high level, and they did not have the capital to become farmers. They were left only with menial, low-paying jobs that were not going to lead to any degree of affluence in industry, commerce, or agriculture. The only legitimate route open to them was politics. This is the real key to the American Irish. Most of our immigrants came to these shores in search of freedom or of the right to practice their own religion or to take advantage of economic opportunities for which they *were* already prepared. The Irish—like my great grandfather—came here because they wanted a square meal. There was no way of getting it except through taking over governmental agencies.

In doing so, however, they not only seized power but put the stamp of Irish Ethos on politics. They were pragmatic—a group of men and women who thought of government as a means of making a living rather than a vehicle for promoting an ideology. They cared little about the so-called substantive issues but a lot about the plight of people who were hard up.

It was this discovery that led to my strong interest in the past of the Irish. They brought certain talents to the political and governing process—talents that had been developed by the long struggle for survival in Ireland. It is these characteristics which I wish to set forth in this book.

Chapter 2

♣

The FORGING of a NATION

ONE OF THE MAJOR REWARDS IN STUDYING HISTORY IS THE DIS-covery that great historical forces usually have trivial beginnings. Nowhere is this better illustrated than in the landing of a small group of Norman knights and men-at-arms at what is now called Baginbun Head, County Wexford, in May of 1170. They were an advance party in the service of the Earl of Pembroke, usually called Strongbow, a Norman-Welsh baron whose loyalty was owed to Henry II, King of England. However, he seems to have been operating on his own rather than as an agent of the English crown. He quickly gathered together some more knights and archers and joined the invasion forces after a few weeks.

This was not the first invasion of Ireland. No one can really be sure as to who first occupied the island although there is evidence that it was inhabited as early as 8000 B.C. But most of what is known about its ancient times comes through stories and songs handed down by word of mouth through itinerant storytellers. They cover people known as Firbolgs, Tuatha Ta Danaan, Fomorians, and the Milesians. For imaginative men and women, they provide marvelous material for whiling away the time on a rainy afternoon when the television set has broken down, and it is necessary to fall back on books for entertainment. For historians, their only value is that they afford clues to the Irish character. The key point is that the *seanachies* (the bards) treated them all as warlike invaders taking the land away from each other. The stories cannot even be checked against the accounts of the Romans, whose occupation of England did not include trips to Ireland or Scotland.

The Gaelic invasion—which gave the people their language —came in the first century A.D. and was supplemented by what may well be called the Christian invasion, under Saint Patrick, in

[15]

the fifth century. The Viking invasion, which gave many people, including me, their "Irish" names, came in the eighth century. But none of these had the lasting impact of the Norman raids spearheaded by Strongbow. The reason was simple. With the exception of Christianity, none of the earlier invaders were able to establish hegemony over the entire island.

It should be said that to classify Strongbow as an invader is to stretch the meaning of the word. Actually, he was invited to enter the country by Dermot Macmurrough, the King of Leinster who was engaged in a fierce battle with other Kings. He was desperate for Norman arms to aid his cause, because armor and bows and arrows were advanced military technology in a land where the deadliest weapon available to warriors was a slingshot. With Norman backing, Macmurrough easily defeated his opponents, but the cost was a beachhead for later invasions and a decision by Strongbow to settle down and stay where he was. He himself became King of Leinster—a position which served him as a base for raids throughout the countryside. Eventually, Henry II decided that the Earl of Pembroke was getting too big for his britches. Taking the position that all of these actions were being performed by his vassal, the English monarch laid claim to all of Ireland. Thus began a struggle that was to last for nearly eight centuries and scatter the Irish people all over the world. Obviously, this account is simply a once-over-lightly, which will leave both historians and students of mythology unsatisfied. For our purposes, however, it is sufficient to make the major point essential to this book—that there was no such thing as an Irish state, or even a province, until the English took over. What really existed were warring families, some of which had extended control over several counties. But none of them, including the semilegendary high king, Brian Boru, ever succeeded in taking over the whole island. There was no unity whatsoever beyond the loyalty to the clan. The popular pub song "A Nation Once Again" is like many pub songs, inaccurate. "A Nation at Last" would correspond better with history. Before Strongbow, the Irish had a common language and a common religion, but there was no form of political or economic unity.

Other Norman forces poured into Ireland by way of the stronghold erected originally by Strongbow and scattered across the island. But something seemed to happen to them once they crossed the Irish Sea and were separated from London by water. They became more Irish than the Irish and joined into the inter-tribal struggles. The Norman de Burgos became Burke, and Fitz (*fils*, son of) names were scattered all over the landscape. Technically, their fealty was to the English crown, but the reality was a series of alliances with Gaelic chieftains. A Parliament meeting under royal auspices at Kilkenny in 1366 actually tried to legislate against the wearing of Irish clothing and Irish hairstyles by "the English born in Ireland." The act accomplished nothing. Whatever the British King might claim, his influence was actually limited to "the Pale"—an area of a few hundred square miles around Dublin.

For at least three centuries, the political life of Ireland could best be described as a slightly modified form of anarchy. Subjects of the English crown who lived beyond the Pale paid little attention to London and, at times, conducted themselves in open defiance of their legal master. In 1534 Henry VIII decided that he had had enough. He laid down a law that *all* lands in that nation had to be surrendered to the crown and then have their titles regranted. Henry himself was too busy between multiple marriages and disputes with the Pope and the King of Spain to ride herd on the execution of the act. But it was passed on to his daughter, Elizabeth I, a woman who was quite capable of following through on any activity. She enforced the law with severity, sending British-born agents into every county and dismissing the older Anglo-Irish. She also sent in British-born soldiers, who displayed no mercy in punishing or executing anyone who resisted.

There were rebellions, the last one of importance led by Hugh O'Neill, Earl of Tyrone, who actually succeeded in defeating an English army. But it was the last gasp. Elizabeth had brought the whole island under control. It was now a part of England—of course, a subordinate part—and there was no doubt as to who was running the show. An unexpected result of the Elizabethan victory—at first apparently unimportant—was the appearance of a unifying force in Irish politics: hatred of the English. The people were converted from a loose collection of warring tribes to a society with a mission—to shake off the hated rule of alien conquerors.

It is something of a paradox that the factors that had made defeat at the hands of the English inevitable became a source of strength once English rule was established. During the struggle Irish armies were bested in almost every battle, because they were basically ad hoc alliances of men and women whose emotional priorities were vested in the family. When they fought, it was as a collection of groups who had no experience in fighting as a disciplined force. It was very simple for the trained forces of England to split them into small units, which could be eliminated at leisure. There was heroism in the resistance, but wars are won by soldiers rather than heroes.

When the resistance was shifted from the battlefield to the streets, a different set of forces came into play. Family ties can be very close without any formal structure being involved. With few exceptions, no one has to draw up a set of by-laws to govern family life. Most important of all, when family life is healthy, there is no need for courts to try people or formal punishments to correct misdoing. Ostracism is a sanction so potent that very few men and women—at least in the sixteenth, seventeenth, eighteenth, and nineteenth centuries—would risk it.

What this meant was that the Irish clan system adapted the people to guerrilla warfare. Clan members could associate with each other without appearing to be plotting against authority. Quick decisions could be made that did not require record-making transmission. Cooperation was assured, and the best possible defense against treachery was already in place—ostracism. None of this had been very helpful as long as the clans fought each other. But once united by hatred of a common enemy, it was potent indeed.

The ability to conduct organized activity without organization was not the only fallout of English rule. Queen Elizabeth and her successors had no such intention, but the most important result of their oppressions may well have been the creation of an Irish consciousness. Before Henry VIII, the people of the island identified themselves primarily as followers of a tribal chieftain. After Queen Elizabeth, they became Irishmen and Irishwomen—a transition that was bound to have consequences.

Modern Irishmen attribute their togetherness to Celtic descent. I will never forget a meeting I attended with Tommy Corcoran—one of the Roosevelt advisers who supposedly had "a passion for anonymity"—and a couple of other men with Irish names. We had come together to discuss strategy for launching a Johnson-for-President boom, and Tommy opened the meeting by saying: "We're all Celts here, and we don't have to worry about anyone else listening. We can lay our cards on the table." I started to say: "Hey, Tommy. All of us got here via Ireland, but I want a look at your stud book before you can convince me that you're a Celt." However, I decided that discretion was the better part of valor and we got to work. I could not quite see the relevance of labeling the Milesians, Danes, Vikings, and Normans—not to mention whatever really existed in terms of Firbolgs, Fomorians, and Tuatha Ta Danaan—as Celts. But everyone in the room understood American politics, and it turned out to be a good session.

One other aspect of the results of English rule should also be mentioned. It was what can be termed the Irish diaspora—the dispersal of the Irish throughout the world. It meant Irish in France (Marshal MacMahon and Hennessey brandy), in Chile (whose liberator and first President was Bernardo O'Higgins), in Argentina (where a Lynch started the line that led to Che Guevara), and to virtually every point on the globe where opportunity existed for men and women with wit and audacity. It would be wide of the mark to think in terms of an Irish international. But it did illustrate the fantastic adaptability of the Irish to other economic and social climates. In every nation they visited, they quickly became potent forces in the administration of the government.

As for the Irishmen who remained in Ireland, the battle for

survival became a matter of sullen resistance and quiet sabotage. It was not planned nor was it dramatic. But the British found it far more difficult to handle than the Irish armies. The latter could be dispensed by a whiff of grapeshot or a charge of heavily armed dragoons. But cannon and sabers were of little use in getting the maximum yield from a field of barley or keeping cows from breaking down fences and chewing up grain. Had the English agents thought in terms of some kind of accommodation, the subsequent history might have been far different. But their minds were set solely on enforcement and repression.

In Ireland, wealth was in the land, and English intentions focused on means of controlling that wealth. What evolved was a landlord-tenant system in which all the cards were stacked in favor of the landlord. The Irish tenant paid rent to a landlord (who often lived in London, which meant that the rents were paid to his representative) for the privilege of a crude hut in which to live and the right to grow crops. In most instances, the amount of the rent was set at the end of the crop year—always close to the sums gained by selling the crop and often at the exact amount. In short, the tenant had worked the whole year for the privilege of having a place to live. However, he was also entitled to one-quarter acre for subsistence. This was the origin of the affiliation between the Irish and the potato. A huge amount of them can be grown on a quarter acre.

Placing the land firmly in the hands of men loyal to the English crown reached its ultimate form in a plan drafted in London between 1608 and 1610. It was an effort to establish an "Ulster plantation" in the counties of Donegal, Tyrone, Derry, and Armagh—the seats of Hugh O'Neill and Rory O'Donnell, the last two serious Irish Catholic opponents of British rule. To the four counties was to be added Cavan and Fermanagh, and the whole was to become a colonization area for British and Scots Protestant settlers, who were to be brought directly from their homelands. The settlers, with the exception of a small number of veteran soldiers, were to be forbidden to rent their land to Irish tenants, and about 10 percent of the poorest land was reserved for the Irish, who would pay double the normal rent to the crown.

Very few plans on such a grandiose scale ever work out, and this was no exception. Many of the Irish who were scheduled to be ousted managed to stay, in order to provide services for the new landlords. The proposal did not turn out to be as attractive to the English as it was to the Scots, who came in droves. But the basic concept of establishing Ulster as a Protestant, pro-British enclave held, and the fighting that it brought about has remained to plague England to this day. What is far more important, it had an impact upon Irish emigrants, which was to be reflected in the United States many years later.

The fundamental and longest-lasting result of the Ulster project was that it politicized religion. Suddenly, Protestantism became something much more to the Irish peasant than a set of beliefs with which he disagreed. It became the symbol for depriving him of his land, if he still held any, or of increasing his rents beyond all bounds if he had been reduced to tenancy. Before the project, Protestants were simply people who were damned to eternal fires. That was their business. If they wanted to go to hell, no Irishman was going to stand in their way. But when they wanted to take Irish land with them on the trip, that was serious. Such an act automatically labeled Protestantism as "the enemy" and Protestant ministers as the minions of English landlords.

When it comes to gauging the depth of Irish enmity to Protestantism, one must proceed with great care. It was not an enmity that was shared by Irish intellectuals. When we run over the names of the men who "led the battle for Irish freedom," it is possible to go through more than three centuries without finding more than a few who were Catholic. Wolfe Tone, Robert Emmet, Charles Stewart, Thomas Parnell were Protestants, who had become so because it was a path to education in Ireland. They were quite capable of distinguishing between the acts committed by the state and the acts committed by the state under the guise of religion.

To the Irish peasant, there was no distinction. He knew that

[21]

he had lost both rights and land because he was a Catholic and that the rights and the land had been given to others because they were Protestant. The political machinery fashioned by the Irish *after* they had reached the United States originated with *these very Irish peasants*—mostly from the agrarian counties of the west. The intellectuals have left us a rich legacy of lore and literature. But the ultimate political effectiveness rested with the men who raised barley for the landlords and potatoes for themselves.

By the mid-1850s, the Irish character had been formed. It had little or nothing, outside the confines of Dublin, to do with Cu Chulain or Fionn Mac Cumhail. But it had plenty to do with two centuries of struggling for survival in an environment where every Irishman was constantly on the thin edge of disaster. Those who survived were lean and mean. They were quick of wit and masters of dissembling. They understood political leverage and knew when to attack, when to retreat, and when to hide. Above all, they were the world's greatest experts in the art of warfare without confrontation. They could make alliances without formal conferences, agreements, or treaties that would leave a record. They could act in concert without giving commands but with a clear understanding of who was in charge. These were the lessons they had learned while living under repression. It did not take them very long to learn how to apply their underground tactics to a democracy.

Chapter 3

♣

A SQUARE MEAL

THE IRISH POTATO FAMINE IMMIGRANTS THAT FLOODED THESE shores between 1847 and 1853 were different from earlier Irish immigrants, as well as from the rest of the American populace, because of their experience of fleeing from disaster. They were fugitives from horror, and the words "immigration" or "emigration" did not really apply to them. It was a mass *migration* to countries where they hoped to find a meal.

The migration was not limited to the United States. Many of them went to Australia or to Latin America. But the vast majority came to the United States because the length of the travel was relatively short. As a sidelight, many of them (including my great-grandfather) came to Canada, because steerage fare to Montreal was cheap. But the British flag flew over Canada, and memories were bitter. Significant numbers of them set out for the United States as soon as they could.

There were relatively sizable Irish immigrations long before the late 1840s. New York City's St. Patrick's Day parade is older than the U.S. Constitution, proof that there were ample Irish there before the Revolution. The blight which caused the famine struck potato crops briefly in the 1820s and the 1830s. But it was not as devastating in those years as it became at the century's midpoint. There was a constant passage of individuals—mostly from Northern Ireland—moved by a desire for economic opportunity, a yearning for political freedom, or a search for religious tolerance. In addition, there were Irish revolutionaries. There had been no major armed uprisings since 1798, but the Act of Union binding England and Ireland had not pacified the Irish temperament, and unrest was rampant.

Exact figures are unobtainable, and even acknowledged authorities such as William V. Shannon and Cecil Woodham-Smith can only give estimates. But it is safe to say that Irish immigration in the 1820s, 1830s, and early 1840s came out to about 35,000 a year—an *average* figure, not a constant. As early as 1809 Irish names, such as Patrick McKay, began to bob up in Tammany Hall, and in 1817 that venerable organization found itself confronted with a demand to nominate Thomas Addis Emmet for Congress. In the 1840s, an Irish-born journalist named Mike Walsh shook up Tammany Hall by organizing a group called the Spartan Association and campaigning for honesty in New York City government. He wound up in the state legislature and was elected to the U.S. Congress in 1852. These, however, were mere episodes, and Emmet and Walsh could have had the same careers had they been named Schultz and Smythe. They did not serve as the launching pad for what we now consider the Irish political machines. That had to wait for the great famine, which almost overnight changed the complexion of urban America.

From the late 1840s to the Civil War, about 1,700,000 left Ireland for the United States. The peak year was 1851 with an Irish immigration on the magnitude of 220,000—mostly from western and southwestern Ireland. The history of this tremendous movement of people has been covered fully in the classic books *The American Irish* by Shannon and *The Great Hunger* by Woodham-Smith. What is at issue here is its impact on the American political system.

Certain realities of the migration must be cited. The most important single fact is, as we have noted, that they came to the United States in a desperate search for food. Other immigrants came hunting political or religious freedom or, at least, economic opportunity. The pragmatic Irish immigrants of the 1840s and 1850s were not concerned with ideology. They were ready to make a deal with anyone as long as it put meat and potatoes on the table.

Second in importance is that genuine economic opportunity —of the kind that had been available to the earlier immigrants— really did not exist for them. They had no capital which would

[26]

have enabled them to become farmers, the only occupation at which they possessed some skills. The potato blight had exercised its most devastating impact upon the poorest sections of Ireland, where education had been overlooked for centuries, and they lacked job training that today we would consider elementary. In short, nothing was open to them except "muscle" work at the lowest level of the social ladder.

Third, they were Catholics set adrift in a land where the established settlers were not only Protestant but, all too often, Protestants who had inherited a virulent form of anti-Catholicism. In addition to the religious identification, there was also a cultural dissimilarity best expressed in the use of English as a language. To WASP America, their accents at best were funny and at worst incomprehensible. The Irish were regarded as an indigestible lump who were secret agents of the Pope (known to many as the Whore of Rome) and were incapable of any words other than "Faith and Begorrah."

Finally, they also brought with them what turned out to be a major asset. It was the Irish clan system that welded them into a community—a community fully capable of acting in concert while disregarding the formal governmental and legal structure without being crushed by it. Seven centuries of life in a land where the laws were made by aliens who sought to keep them supine had left them with only a passing respect for parliaments, city councils, and elections but a fierce loyalty to family ties and interfamilial relationships. About the only educated part of the population of western Ireland consisted of the famous "Limerick lawyers," who drove British judges to madness by their ability to obfuscate every point of law and who could always produce twenty or thirty witnesses willing to swear that their clients had been nowhere near the scene of the crime when it happened (this has gone down in history as the Limerick Alibi).

In short, the Irish in America were a distinguishable group of people living as outsiders in the midst of the heaviest population centers and willing to do just about anything to survive. They were aliens in a sense that went far beyond any of the earlier settlers—

even the Scots who were also Celtic but who were Protestants who had moved into rural areas such as Appalachia where they did not irritate their neighbors (people do not have to live in such close proximity in the mountains). At the same time, however, they were already trained to act as a disciplined army when it came to underground political warfare. It was only a matter of time before they put this skill to use in building city machines, which surpassed in efficiency anything else that the free world has ever known.

The famine Irish reached the United States at a moment in history when a tremendous market was opening up for unskilled labor. This was due to a spurt in the growth of large industrial cities and means of inland transportation. A nation that had been devoted primarily to agriculture and trading was moving into the factory system. This meant a demand for men with strong backs who would work cheap. The Irish were in this category and flocked into the coal mines, the steel mills, and the construction industry. They quickly picked up blue-collar work skills. By 1900, the Irish Americans who were only 7.5 percent of the work force comprised 33 percent of the boilermakers, plumbers, and steamfitters. Similar figures could be cited for virtually every skilled blue-collar occupation.

The most significant development of the second half of the nineteenth century was the heavily increased need for urban security. An industrial society has compelling reasons for police. Factories are more vulnerable to sabotage than farms, and disparate people crowded into a city are more likely to resort to violent confrontations than farmers. In one sense, the Irish Americans were the major contributors to unrest in Boston, New York, Philadelphia, and Chicago. The early gangsters were Irish, and during the Civil War they virtually tore New York apart. As the century wore on, however, they also became the main source of recruiting for urban police forces. There is one fairly respectable —though unprovable—theory that the city fathers deliberately encouraged recruitment of Irish policemen in the belief that only they could control Irish gangs.

The other area of historic importance involves city fire departments. At the end of the eighteenth century, firefighting was a community activity. Neighbors were expected to form bucket brigades to put out conflagrations, and houses were far enough apart that fires were unlikely to wipe out whole townships. As the cities became larger, so did the need for full-time firemen. Again, the Irish took over. The results, at first, were somewhat unusual. Every fire station had some affiliation with an Irish gang. When a fire broke out, contending gangs would appear on the scene and fight for control of fire hydrants, or access to river water. Sometimes the building would burn down before control could be established. Reading about the episodes a century later, they seem somewhat comic. But it is doubtful whether the anxious householder found anything amusing in his property going up in smoke while Clancys, Kellys, McGuires, and Skeffingtons wrestled each other.

The social sciences had not been born at that point, and it is consequently uncertain just how the Irish took over the police and fire departments. But the forces that brought about the takeover are unimportant. The fact is that it happened. The concept of the "Irish cop" became deeply ingrained in our society. Police vans for hauling suspects are still called "Paddy wagons," because the men who drove them were Irish and a plain clothes detective is still known as a "shamus" (after the Irish Seamus for James). The point becomes crystal clear when one examines the lists of police and fire commissioners in major cities in the late 1800s. It is almost impossible to find one without an Irish name.

Putting everything together, the picture that emerges is one of an easily definable minority acquiring influence out of all proportion to its numbers and achieving this by controlling the nerve points of an expanding society: Did you want to remodel your house? If so, you had to deal with skilled carpenters, masons, and bricklayers who were mostly Irish. Were you a housewife whose plumbing was out of whack? If so, you had to call a plumber whose name would begin with a "Mc" or an "O'" and whose brogue would be so thick as to justify the term "flannel mouth." Was your house on fire? The only possible rescue would be Celtic.

Was your kid run in for pinching apples from a fruit stand? If so, you dealt with a blue-eyed, red-headed cop who could be *very* understanding to "nice" people.

In Ireland, this could not have happened. There all social questions had been settled by people who had power before the Industrial Revolution had even started and who lived on another island. The rulers could—and did—sustain their sovereignty by force of arms. The policemen were either British soldiers or a constabulary which was overseen by British soldiers. The Limerick lawyers might drive the British judges to a frenzy, but they could not get rid of those judges or shake off the power which they represented.

The United States, however, was going through a period of transition. This meant that the Irish had something to offer in a nation where there was no absolute, rigid, repressive social structure except for blacks. This left the Potato Famine Gaels and their descendants free to probe the vulnerable points of WASP society and to move into areas which they could preempt. The Irish talent of working together *outside the law but without disturbing the laws* could be exercised with awesome effect. Their neighbors might not like them, but they had to deal with them. There was no alternative.

As the century wore on, another factor came into being. It was the mass migration of other immigrants who were neither WASP nor Scots. There were Polish, Italians, Germans, Swedes, and Russian Jews fleeing pogroms. The Germans and the Swedes could take fairly good care of themselves. But the eastern and southern nationalities were of a different stripe. They were as alien to the United States as the Irish, and they did not even have the advantage of speaking English. For a variety of reasons, they lacked the Irish ability to act as a community in taking over social choke points. Therefore, they needed friends. The Irish were willing to help them out (for a price in terms of votes) and to give them some introduction to life in America. The Irish machines actually drew their strength from performing social services for the immigrants.

The attitude of the Irish toward immigrants of other nationalities could not be described as benevolent. They did not hate Italians, Jews, and Poles the way they hated the English. But they were certainly the leaders in fostering the mythology of ethnic warfare. The derogatory terms "Wop," "Sheeny," "Polack," and "Hunky" were common currency in the social discussions of the near North Side during my boyhood. It was taken for granted that "Dagos" carried knives but were fistless, "Heebs" made their living by cheating Christians, and Eastern Europeans were nasty drunks who did not imbibe joyfully as did the "Micks."

These attitudes should have resulted in endless bickering, which would prevent any access to political power by the ethnic groups. At this point, however, Irish practicality took over. After all, no matter how the various nationalities felt about each other, they still shared a common foe—the dominant WASPs. Kelly might not like Basile; Cohen might regard Clancy as a lazy loafer; Visznitski might choke with loathing on sighting De Marco. But those were just emotions. They did not go as deep as the yearning for jobs and social respectability. This meant that the "organization" could put together tickets on election day that gave a little something to everybody. The coalescing channel was the Irish.

What made the whole thing possible was the fact that "the organization" had no interest in political principles. Politics were not conducted as a means of translating ideological concepts into working programs. Instead, the point of the whole process was to find orderly methods of parceling out the economic benefits of society. At heart, boodlery, which governed the urban political process, was the Irish formula for redistribution of the wealth. One of its advantages was that all of the ethnic groups could subscribe to it, whereas they would have been split all over the city in contests over "substantive" issues.

The "melting pot" idea is one dear to the American heart. We have been boasting throughout this century of our ability to bring divergent cultures together so people could live in peace and harmony within one nation. To a great extent (if one closes one's eyes to the present-day lot of blacks and Latin Americans) the concept is valid. It is little short of amazing that we have assimilated so many diverse ethnic groups in a democratic society. However, we have not explored with any degree of realism the factors that made our unity possible. In the early days of our Republic, of course, people did not live so closely together that they would get on each other's nerves. But in the big cities, different conditions prevailed. Immigrants found themselves jammed into tenements already occupied by immigrants who did not even speak the same language. What was the process that enabled them to work together?

There is no simple answer to this question, but I believe that one of the most important factors was the Irish political machine. It was crooked; it was crude; it was vulgar. But it also worked out a common denominator for the ethnic groups. A country is not a nation until it has found a means of bringing diverse people together for a common cause. Somehow, divisive issues must be swept under the rug until citizens become accustomed to working together. In countries like Russia, this was done by adopting the principle of absolutism for the ruler and keeping the different elements of Russian society from each other's throats by quieting them through military power. In India the unity comes from an inaction amounting almost to paralysis on most issues. In the United States, we found part of our unity through the Irish political machine.

Chapter 4

♣

The PROMISED LAND

THE UNITED STATES TO WHICH HUNGRY MIGRANTS CAME WAS going through one of the most sweeping transitions of the nineteenth century. Even the era of Andrew Jackson, which brought the "common man" into the political arena, did not go as far in revolutionizing the social structure. It had enfranchised poor farmers from the Appalachian and prairie regions, thus putting an end to government by an Eastern elite. But the basic character of the nation was still shaped by the economics of production and export of agricultural products and raw materials. This was reflected in a series of political battles to keep a balance between commerce and farming. The years of the late 1840s and the 1850s saw much more than the introduction of new elements into that struggle. The whole political process was put on a different plane.

A look at the economic picture makes the point. From 1848 to 1860 the most compelling fact in American life was the Industrial Revolution. Some 21,000 miles of railroad track were laid; the production of anthracite coal—used almost entirely by heavy industry—jumped from 4,327,000 short tons to 10,984,000 short tons in ten years, and the Patent Office went from an average annual issue of 527 (1832 to 1849) to an average per year of 1,959 for the decade. Factories had existed in the United States but not on the scale of the mid-1800s. An accumulation of small establishments created an economy in which the process of industrialization suddenly burgeoned. With the change in the economy came a rapid deterioration in the political system. It was one of the most inglorious periods of American governmental and political history.

The years that had preceded 1848 were memorable for political leaders who even today are regarded as giants—Webster, Clay, Calhoun, Jackson, Polk, Benton, and many others. These

[35]

men had succeeded in holding the Union together without resort to arms despite the explosive issue of slavery. Whether they could have done so longer is problematical. But the fact remains that their successors were not of their caliber. As for the Presidents, anyone who, without checking an almanac, can name those that presided during the 1850s is either a scholar of the American Presidency or an expert in trivia quiz games. They were Fillmore, Pierce, and Buchanan—names that are on every historian's list of the ten worst Chief Executives.

The Democratic Party split along North–South lines (with most of its strength in the South) and the Whig Party disappeared altogether. A number of strange-sounding groups tried to enter the scene—the Conscience Whigs, the Loco Focos, the Barn Burners, and the Native American Party. The latter, usually known as the Know-Nothings, concentrated its efforts on banning further Irish immigration and expelling the Irish who were already here. It achieved some degree of success in electing members to Congress (usually, however, not under the name of the party itself but as members of some other group), and Fillmore ran for reelection under its banner—but only after the Whigs showed good judgment in making him the first sitting President to be denied renomination by his own party. The compelling issue was not slavery per se but the extension of slave territory, and this is what eventually brought about the formation of the Republican Party and the return of some political stability.

One important factor at work—although not yet apparent—was the urbanization of American society. The world of the early nineteenth century was distinctly rural, and the whole orientation of economic life was toward agriculture—either servicing the farm regions or distributing their products. Cities existed, of course, since there was a need for ports. But there was no doubt as to where the control forces were lodged. In 1830, less than one tenth of the people of the United States lived in urban surroundings, and only New York City could number its population at over 200,000. The major political battles were not between the cities and the farms, but between the slave-operated plantations and the family-owned "free soil" farms. State legislatures saw to it that the "city slickers" did not get out of hand.

In the 1850s, urbanization, with a resultant power shift, was becoming apparent. Industrialization had proceeded to a point where it was straining to operate with insufficient manpower. A factory system, at least in its early stages of development, requires large pools of labor, which can be hired in a hurry when orders are high and fired just as fast when orders taper off. Those pools must have containers, and this means that the workers must have housing in close proximity to factories—in other words, there must be cities.

As many writers have pointed out, the times were marked by a major paradox. The Famine Irish were basically farmers. For generations about all they had known—other than periods of service as mercenary soldiers—was farming the land. The Sons of the Mil had built no cities, not even Dublin, which was erected by the Danes. But in the United States they became factory workers and city dwellers. About the closest they came to life in a rural area were the small towns of Appalachia where they found jobs as coal miners.

It is idle to speculate on what would have happened had the famine sufferers arrived in the United States during an earlier era, when life was stable. In reality, many Irish did, and the early history of the nation is studded with names like Thomas Fitzsimmons and the first Pierce Butler (both signers of the Constitution), John Barry and Richard Montgomery, all Irish-born. But these, by and large, were the Anglo-Irish—men of education who differed from the other settlers only in terms of religion. They made no basic changes in the American system of government and politics.

In retrospect, the disabilities of the Famine Irish may have given them a certain "edge." They had nothing to unlearn, no well-established farms to abandon. These hungry men driving spikes on the railroad, rolling steel in a mill, or digging coal out of the mines did not have to make any choice between such work and a more leisurely way of life. Their only options were to sign the payroll and eat or not sign it and starve. They were desperate, and

[37]

desperation leads people to try anything—even though it may be unpleasant.

Had the famine sufferers arrived earlier, they might not have had any choice at all. They were totally unskilled in any occupation other than low-level farming, and there were black slaves to do that. Of course, the women could do some household work and some ditches had to be dug. But that was not enough to provide any sort of economic life. The instability of the United States in the mid-nineteenth century was a two-sided coin. On the one hand, it was upsetting our social, economic, and political life. But on the other it was providing opportunity for people who needed it badly.

One cannot avoid asking why other immigrant groups who entered in the mid-nineteenth century did not make forays into politics as did the Irish. Large numbers of Germans came over about the same time as a result of the unsuccessful revolutions that swept Central Europe in 1848. These immigrants, however, were looking for freedom and opportunity, and they had high degrees of skill in such trades as farming, construction, and brewing. They were important factors in the foundation of such cities as St. Louis and Milwaukee. But they did not regard themselves as rejects— merely as men and women who had lost a political argument. They beefed up the antislavery forces in the United States, and, of course, they gained political control in localities where they were domi- nant. But they already had ways to make a living. They did not look upon government simply as a source for jobs.

Furthermore, some of these new immigrants had financial backing. They could strike out for the interior of the country, where there was plenty of fertile land, because they had the re- sources to outfit themselves or were sponsored by wealthy bene- factors. Typical of these are the *Landsleute* in Texas, who located first in San Antonio and then moved into the Hill Country, where they settled isolated villages in which their children could retain their Germanic identity. They were sponsored by a liberal German prince—Otto Karl von Braunfels von Solms—after whom a num- ber of small communities were named. These Germans established such towns as Fredericksburg, New Braunfels, Bandera and Seguin, and like everyone who attempts to settle a frontier, they worked hard. But thanks to the generosity of their benefactor, their resources for coping with the wilderness were adequate. Similar conditions existed in Wisconsin, Iowa, Missouri and many parts of the middle west.

This was denied to the Irish. What little money they could bring with them from Ireland was usually exhausted before they even left the boat. It cost some money to move off the East Coast and plunge into the interior. The pioneer and his family had to have a wagon, horses, tools, at least a shotgun, cooking utensils, bedding, clothing, and some medicines. One need not be a millionaire to take Horace Greeley's advice and "go west." But a stake was necessary. What was also necessary was the ability to manage a homestead farm. It was doubtful whether very many of the Potato Famine refugees had the necessary knowledge and skill. Their farming experience had been a variety of sharecropping, and all they really knew was how to work—under direction—land belonging to somebody else and how to raise a quarter acre of potatoes.

For people at the very bottom of the social and economic ladder, the big cities are the only available habitat in which it is possible to live. A metropolitan area is no place for raising food, but it does afford opportunities for scrounging. Someone is always throwing away stale food. There are trash heaps, where people discard wornout clothes. There are always slum neighborhoods, where rickety, vermin-infested buildings offer cheap lodgings. Quick pickup jobs are available in cities: chopping wood, running errands, holding horses, cleaning out privies, shoveling snow, sweeping chimneys, and doing all the dirty work that comfortable householders abhor. It was natural that the Irish should stay in the cities.

More important than all of the factors we have just named, however, is the role of the city as the most potent mechanism for social change. People who are living so closely together become dependent upon each other and must adjust their conduct to the state of their society. In a rural, or semirural, society, eccentricity flourishes because it doesn't endanger other people unless it is extreme and far-reaching. Nobody is going to stop a farmer from building a privy near his own drinking water supply. Nobody is going to insist on elaborate traffic patterns for a small town, where most transportation is on foot. The situation changes radically, however, in a large city where technological advance is going to have an impact upon life-styles and where eccentricities can endanger the people in a whole neighborhood. The result is that cities undergo a constant readjustment. They are nerve centers for our whole society and register changes ahead of the other areas. The reason the ambitious young stream to New York or Boston or Chicago or Denver or Los Angeles is that the big cities are where constant change means constantly renewing opportunity.

The conditions of life for the Potato Famine immigrants could be summed up in one word—horrible. They were jammed into the slums, and the religious hostility was beyond what they had known before. The British government had placed Catholics in a disadvantaged economic position, but that was not quite the same thing as the savage bigotry of American Protestants. Typical was the book *Awful Disclosures of the Hotel Dieu in Montreal*, which circulated throughout the United States, spreading the belief that nuns were really prostitutes for priests. The result of this type of discrimination was a tendency on the part of the American-Irish to be more "Catholic" than the Irish-Irish. Thus the fierce devotion of the American-Irish led to Irish domination of the Catholic Church in all major American cities. The Irish priest became as much a stereotype as the Irish policeman, and every joke about the Catholic clergy began "Father Gilligan" or "Father Kelly" or "Father O'Brien." Under these circumstances, it was inevitable that the Church should become identified with big-city politics as the Irish rose to political control. An unexpected fallout came when Catholic immigrants from southern and eastern Europe began to enter the United States in large numbers. To control the religion of a people is to exercise an advantage in leading them.

The depressed conditions under which the Irish immigrants lived was one of the factors that led to their ultimate political success. In Ireland, they were held together by the clan system, but the clans were not very good at cooperating with one another—as was demonstrated by the failure of so many uprisings. In America, the Irish found themselves welded into an army that very quickly acquired discipline and a *community* outlook. A Cohan would never have met a Prendergast in County Clare or County Wicklow, but in New York City or Boston they would have rooms in the same tenement and share the expenses of bringing home beer in the growler. The big city slum led the Irish to do something they had been unable to do all the way back to Strongbow—battle the rest of the world in unity. In a sense, they had to cross the Atlantic Ocean under the worst possible conditions in order to become a nation.

This state of "nationhood" within the United States fostered an exaggerated sense of Irish pride. St. Patrick's Day in Ireland, for example, was originally little more than a Mass. In Boston, New York, and Chicago, it became a major ritual, with parades that no elected politician dared ignore. In Boston, the holiday is official, although the title of the celebration is British Evacuation Day (during the Revolution, British troops evacuated Boston on March 17) to get around the separation of Church and State doctrine. In Chicago, Mayor Daley dyed the waters of the city's rivers a Kelly green. In New York City, the Fifth Avenue traffic lines are painted green, and every public character suddenly discovers a Celtic ancestor somewhere among his or her forebears in order to join the procession. In recent years the cities of Ireland have swung around to celebrating the day on the American model.

There is also a mythology for the American Irish. One of the more famous examples was the sign "No Irish Need Apply," which allegedly adorned the Boston pier in the last part of the nineteenth century. Persistent research has failed to uncover actual evidence that the sign existed on the pier, although it was probably in the windows of nearby houses. But almost any American with an Irish name will tell you that his grandfather either saw it across the pier entrance or told him that his great-grandfather had seen it. (In my case, it was my grandfather on my mother's side who told me that his father had seen it.) I have never been able to nail down positive proof that it existed or did not exist. But it has the unifying character that comes with being believed. Its physical existence is irrelevant.

Had the social system remained static, the Irish diaspora would have remained tragic. But the United States was undergoing what may have been the greatest change in its whole history. This was reflected in the rapid growth of the big cities. In 1840, Boston had a population of 93,000. Ten years later, it had grown to over 136,000. During the same period, Providence, Rhode Island, went from 23,000 to 41,000, Philadelphia from 220,000 to 340,000, and New York City from 312,000 to 515,000. The Irish stayed in—or traveled to—urban centers, adding to population growth and the problems that came with that growth. In the past, many immigrants had just passed through the port cities on their way to small towns or farm lands in the interior. The Irish did not pass through. They became the backbone of the industrial areas.

Chapter 5
♣
The
LUMPENPROLETARIAT

A QUICK EXAMINATION OF THE FAMINE IRISH IN THE 1850S AND early 1860s brings to mind a phrase used over and over by Karl Marx—*die Lumpenproletariat*. These were the outcasts of society—the unskilled, unprincipled, thieving droves of riffraff, who had no hope for the future. Marx looked upon the Lumpens as a barrier to social change, who had no relationship to the blue-collar workers upon whom he based his prescription for the rectification of social evils.

The most visible form of Irish activity in the United States was gangsterism. These young toughs were the backbone of such famed groups as the Bowery Boys, the Roach Guards, and the Dead Rabbits. They were produced by the same conditions that have brought about the emergence of the black and Hispanic gangs of modern times—young, restless men living in conditions of misery from which there seems to be no escape. They had grudges against the largely WASP society into which they had come, and they took every opportunity they could find to terrorize "respectable" people. In terms of financial remuneration, few, if any, of the gangsters or their leaders reaped sizable rewards. But they had the deep satisfaction of seeing the spasm of fear that would flash on elite faces that had spotted a couple of hoodlums walking down the block. It was some compensation for being poor.

The problem of the Irish gangsters reached serious proportions during the Civil War. The federal government decided to resort to conscription for its armies in 1863, and in the summer of that year the terms were announced in New York City. They included a provision whereby someone who had been selected for military service could buy his way out for a payment of $300—a sum beyond the reach of anyone who lived in the Bowery or

[45]

along Mulberry Street. To Potato Famine victims, this was another example of Sassenachs living at ease while the Irish did their dirty—and dangerous—work. The gangs quickly assembled, and treated New York to four days of the bloodiest urban carnage in the city's history.

Mobs estimated at 5,000 to 10,000 people assembled in mid-Manhattan and took virtual control of the streets. A number of buildings were looted and burned, including the Draft Headquarters on Third Avenue, the State Armory at Second Avenue and 21st Street, and a munitions factory a block away. The rioters were after guns and ammunition, and they demonstrated quickly that they knew how to use them. At least eighteen innocent blacks were lynched from lampposts and trees, the Orphan Asylum for Colored Children was burned (mostly by drunken women), and a number of policemen and soldiers—including an infantry colonel—were killed.

The police were totally overwhelmed and federal troops—including artillery units—had to be brought in, fresh from the battle of Gettysburg. The casualties—at least 2,000 dead and 8,000 wounded—were as high as those at the battle of Shiloh or Bull Run. Even though the fighting was finally brought to an end by the military, the New York City authorities came to the conclusion that they still had to deal with the uprising. They appropriated money to buy off from the draft poor people who could not afford to do so themselves.

An interesting indication of the causes for the riots came in an address by Archbishop Hughes seeking to calm the rioters: "I have been hurt by the report that you were rioters," he told a Catholic assemblage at Madison Avenue and 36th Street. "You cannot imagine that I could hear these things without being grievously pained. Is there not some way by which you can stop these proceedings and support the laws, none of which have been enacted against you as Irishmen and Catholics?"

The gangsterism continued after the Civil War. Herbert Asbury, in his book *The Gangs of New York*, printed a page of pictures of leaders of the WHYOs, whom he identified as the most

[46]

savage of all. The names are a giveaway—Farrell, Corcoran, Connolly, Ryan, Hurley, Doyle, Lloyd, Hines, and another Connolly. This was the face of Ireland. For the public, the standard caricature of the Irishman was an apelike creature, long upper lip, pointed teeth, and fringebeard. A modern generation, looking at the famous Nast cartoons attacking Boss Tweed, often misses the point that the characters supporting Tweed were all Irish, portrayed in what had become a classic style.

There was one very important Irish characteristic, however, which took them out of the class of the *Lumpenproletariat*. Marx defined the members of such a group as having no "class consciousness." In the Marxist sense, perhaps the Irish were not "class" conscious, but they were possessed of what might be termed a "Celtic consciousness," which was a more than adequate substitute. It was an identity which gave them high morale, and with that morale a capacity to achieve something other than fire and destruction. They were at the bottom rung of the ladder, but they were bound to start the upward climb.

Pat Moynihan has stated in the book *Beyond the Melting Pot*, which he wrote with Nathan Glazer, that the origins of the Irish political machines can be found in the Irish villages, where the whole town would gather in the local pub for socialization and discussion of problems before the community. I agree with the basic thesis, but believe it must be explored in greater depth. The important point is that in those villages, the inhabitants did not have the *legal* authority to control their own affairs—that was the prerogative of the ruling English. Consequently, not only did the villagers have to find the right answer to their problems, but they also had to work out means of doing what they wanted without provoking retaliation. They became supremely skilled at conducting their own affairs while seeming to leave full authority to a hostile power. Of all the arts they brought from the Old Country, this turned out to be the most useful.

Something else was bred in those village pubs, however. It was a strong sense of morality in terms of the relationships the people had with each other. Laws were merely something that had been enacted for the convenience of the Sassenachs and their police. But clan relationships—and Irish society was built upon the clans—were the binding cement that meant survival. The most despised figure in all Irish literature is The Informer, the monster who betrays his fellow countrymen to the oppressor. There were no binding contracts enforceable in a court of law to hold together men and women scheming to circumvent power. That left only one instrument available for the enforcement of discipline—social ostracism. In a society organized along the lines of family ties, it was a potent instrument indeed. To be isolated from one's family was a one-way ticket to Hell.

There were unexpected side effects to this type of morality. The clan was the basic unit of social organization, and therefore family relationships took on a puritanical tinge. This was reflected in the United States in a Catholic Church dominated by the Irish, which had approximately the same attitude toward sexual ethics as the early Pilgrim Fathers. This, in turn, developed a breed of politician who was virtually ostentatious in his devotion to wife and family and his loathing of extramarital sexual activity. Whatever may have been the realities of their private lives, the picture presented to the public was one of unsullied monogamy. In fairness, it should be said that this was almost certainly more than a pose. Of course, there were backsliders, but in a Celtic matriarchy they would not be many.

Putting all these factors together resulted in a type of Irish character that has charmed some and exasperated others—but also opened the way to slipping through the cracks in society and slowly assuming control. It was compounded of several vital factors: a capacity to unite for action with a minimum of ceremony; an ability to make effective battle plans with only the participants being aware of what was happening; a willingness to junk formal contracts and other legal instruments (which were, after all, only the creations of the Sassenach world); and a fanatical devotion to the sanctity of the pledged word (when given to a fellow-Irishman). I learned early as a child that the most damning thing that could be said about a man was that "he has no word."

To return to the Moynihan thesis, another aspect to village life in Ireland helped educate the descendants of the Potato Famine immigrants to the realities of politics. The discussions that actually settled things for the inhabitants of the village did not take place in city halls or in county courthouses. Their locale was the local pub, where ideas could be tested and compromises explored without premature commitment and without inconvenient interruptions by authority. A constable who dropped by in the evening would find nothing but a group of men discussing the crops and horseflesh between satisfying swigs of dark beer. Before the visit the men at the bar might have been making arrangements for a rent strike or receiving a stand of arms, and the plans could be completed after the constable left. But *authority* would have no information that would enable it to head off the action or trace back the perpetrators.

Conversations in a pub, of course, did not have to be recorded. The agreements existed only in the memories of those who had participated and if one of them should be an informer, it would mean his word against that of everyone else in the room. The custom of strictly verbal agreements that left no incriminating documents behind to make trouble was characteristic of the Irish politicians in America. They abhorred minutes. Martin Lomasney, the boss of West End Boston, laid down his rule for successful politics earlier in this century. "Never write when you can speak; never speak when you can nod," he said.

Of course the conversation might lead to some move in a village or county council. But that would be merely ratification. The mainsprings of power would not be in the chambers of government but in informal gatherings of men who commanded enough loyal followers to put into action the plans they had negotiated with other men of power. The Irish who came to America never mistook politics for a debate process—although debate might be useful at times as a political instrument. They knew that politics was a manipulation of power and that what counted was to locate the centers of such power. These might be far removed from local or national legislatures or even executive mansions.

[49]

Speechmaking was a highly prized art to a people who for several centuries had nothing to put in their bellies but potatoes and conversation, and had become fond of both. But when it came to political power, they were very clear about what had to be done to get it and what could be done with it after it was in their hands.

They were equally clear-eyed on the art of trading favors. There had been very little money in their hands in Ireland, even in the best of times. Much of life consisted of swapping a sack of potatoes for a quantity of wool or plowing a field for a sick neighbor—and thereby putting that neighbor under obligation to repay in some manner. Of course, they had to have something to trade and that was not so easy in the United States—at first. But they were quick at spotting the opportunities that were available. Gradually things opened up. A job at a meat-packing plant in Chicago would give an O'Rourke a chance to get close to the hiring boss and recommend other O'Rourkes (and Kellys, O'Briens, and McMahons too) for a job. This would place all of his beneficiaries under an obligation to support him—perhaps when he ran for shop steward of the local union or, more likely, if he wanted to be a precinct captain or a ward leader. The 1870s, 1880s, and 1890s were periods of economic expansion despite a few recessions, and the workers who had gotten in on the ground floor of the Industrial Revolution were able to take care of their friends.

Of greater importance were the openings on the police and fire departments of the major cities. This was the development that afforded all sorts of trading material. Think of O'Malley walking down the street in his blue uniform with the badge on his chest and swinging his night stick as he walks. There on the corner is Giovanelli with a fruit stand, violating about twenty city ordinances. Is O'Malley going to run him in? Not if he votes right (and promises to clean up his act). Giovanelli might not like O'Malley, and O'Malley might not like Giovanelli. Both of them might go home that night and talk to their wives about "that Mick" or "that Dago." Their kids might even gather some evening for a little social discourse with half-bricks and billies. But that doesn't matter. Giovanelli and O'Malley had a vested interest in each other's well-being, and the process that cemented them together is shot through our society.

Furthermore, no matter how O'Malley may feel about Giovanelli as a person, he knows how to handle their relationship with grace. He is not being "bribed" by Giovanelli, nor is Giovanelli bribing him. They are two independent human beings making a deal which, for all practical purposes, is open and above board. In effect, Giovanelli is taking out a license for exemption from what he regards as nitpicking municipal regulations and is paying for it with his vote. Even-Steven! Later on, if Giovanelli falls on hard times and loses his fruit stand, he may be visited by the precinct captain—let's say a Kelly. Is he going to give Giovanelli charity? Of course not! That would be robbing Giovanelli of his self-esteem. He is there to consummate a deal—a turkey at Thanksgiving and a load of coal for Christmas, and Giovanelli will pay for it with his vote. He will not have to declare poverty on a written form; he will not have to subject his family to prying investigations by case workers; he will not have to explain his possession of family heirlooms (today, a television set). He can hold his head high, because he has merely sold something of value. It is not generally realized now that one of the great strengths of the political machines was their treatment of poor people as human beings rather than "cases."

One other factor must be taken into account. It was a demoralized political party that was in dire need of new blood. The Democratic Party in the North was a major casualty of the Civil War. In the minds of many Americans, it was associated with the Copperheads—those who lived along the borders between the Union and Dixie and had been suspected, both justly and unjustly, of giving aid and comfort to the rebels. It was also the party of agriculture, and its policies were geared to the needs of farmers who had to raise and pay off crop loans every year and who felt oppressed by high interest rates for money. Unfortunately, the War had been touched off by battles between the small family farmer in the North and the slave-owning planters of the South, who had been seeking an extension of slavery into the Western territories.

The Republican Party had been founded primarily on the constituent base of those small farmers. It found its roots in Ohio, Indiana, Illinois, Wisconsin, Nebraska, and parts of Missouri. The successful Union generals during the War had been largely from the Middle West, the men best known and understood by the first Republican President, Abraham Lincoln. The most important point, however, was that wartime success had come to the country under Republican leadership, leaving the party with the prestige that attracts new members. Closely associated with the growth of the party was the formation of the Grand Army of the Republic —the union veterans' organization, which became a potent political factor almost as soon as it was organized.

The Democratic Party still held the allegiance of the South, but that was hardly an asset in the wake of disastrous defeat. It is true that nothing succeeds like success, and nothing fails like failure. And there were relatively few people in the North who wanted to stay on a sinking ship. To add to the Democratic difficulties, southerners converted the party into a device for sustaining racial segregation. This was done by the simple expedient of labeling the party as a private organization, which could exclude anyone it did not like. The next move was to convert the primaries into the real general election, thus permitting the Southern whites to settle all their differences without the intervention of the blacks and then present a united front. The party became famous in many states for placing over its slates a crowing rooster, surrounded by the words "For the Preservation of White Supremacy and Pure White Womanhood."

As a political party, the Republicans did not spend too much time pushing agricultural interests. What followed the Civil War was an era of breathtaking industrial expansion. The dominant elements in a society invariably dominate the successful political parties. The Grand Old Party (GOP) dedicated itself to manufacturing enterprises, and the result was domination of Presidential politics with only two breaks (Grover Cleveland and Woodrow Wilson) in a string of election successes from 1866 to 1932. It managed to hold on to its base among small Northern farmers by the simple expedient of selling them on the high tariff. This was a policy that primarily benefited manufacturing, but only the Southern states—who had a heavy stake in the export markets for cotton, tobacco, and naval stores—protested. Nobody really cared. The South was "out of it."

After the Civil War, the Irish found little welcome in the Republican Party. They were basically muscle workers—the raw human material for manufacturing—and the industrialists who controlled the GOP were interested primarily in keeping their labor costs down. They were in no hurry to enact protective legislation against industrial accidents, and although they appreciated contracts for public works, they did not appreciate city councils who would insist on minimum wage guarantees. It was a period in which very few men wanted to be Democrats, because it did not seem to be a vehicle that could survive. The Irish went into it because there was no alternative organization through which they could exercise their political savvy. And as they were the only sizable group to care about the Democratic Party, they were soon able to shape it into their personal instrument.

At first, the Democratic Party looked like an oxymoron—the party of Southern segregationists and Northern immigrants. In the last part of the nineteenth century, however, that did not matter. The Irish base of the Northern party cared only about the cities in which they lived; even state politics were beyond their horizons. The Southerners had decided (whether consciously or unconsciously) to eschew national politics altogether except as a defense against interference with their racial practices. Consequently, the ex-slave owners went in one direction, and the Irish in another, and the mere fact that they were both traveling under the same label was irrelevant. Down the road it was obvious that there would be a parting of the ways. Political people, however, rarely look down the road because they have too many problems to resolve in the immediate present.

The Democratic Party turned out to be an excellent vehicle for capturing the cities. As time went on, the adulation of the industrialist for the prosperity he was bringing to Americans began to wane. Further immigration increased the labor pool, which helped keep wages at a low level. But it also meant that the industrial workers were growing in their ability to swing elections. There were no restrictions on male use of the franchise in the North, and this led to an increasing tilt of the electoral machinery in metropolitan areas away from the Republican Party that represented the employers. Class consciousness in the United States never reached the levels of intensity that it did in Europe. But the idea that "the workingman" would never get a decent break caught on early. The feeling about employers was easily transferred to the Republican Party, and the urban proletariat moved almost automatically to the opposition. This resulted in a steady growth of Democratically held cities, from 1865 to 1928, while Congress and the White House remained generally Republican. The suburban and small-town middle class tended to sympathize with industry, in alliance with Northern farmers, and since they also sentimental ties to the Union forces of the Civil War, they supported the GOP.

One factor which was not foreseen was that control of the cities would ultimately require the machine bosses to move into state—and ultimately into national—politics. The latter half of the nineteenth century was one in which a majority of Americans still lived in rural areas. Cities had gone past the period in which they were primarily ports and instead had become industrial centers. But they still operated with a high degree of independence. They did not look to state legislatures—let alone to the Federal government—to help them with their problems.

The shift of the population to an economy that was primarily urban changed all this. The city bosses discovered ultimately that they could not service their constituents without going to the state capital and sometimes the United States capital. The lines surrounding metropolitan areas began to blur. But as they blurred, the center of power shifted more and more to the metropolitan

[54]

areas. And who stood at the center of power? The Potato Famine Irish who had entered the Democratic Party on the ground floor and who were now in a position to exercise power. How they did it is a fascinating chapter of American history.

There is, however, one lesson to be drawn from the origins of the machines. When a nation is in a state of transition, there are compensations for living in the lower depths of society. The bottom rung is one from which people are willing to try anything new that offers even a faint hope of rising. The weakness of the Irish was their strength.

Chapter 6

♣

The As *and* Bs *of the* IRISH MACHINES

LIKE MOST COLLEGE GRADUATES MY MEMORIES OF WHAT I learned in school are sporadic. They come—and they go—in flashes, and they leave me to understand that they are there but obtruding on my consciousness only when they are needed. When I began to research this book, the memory of an otherwise forgotten lecture from a political science professor was suddenly pushed to the forefront of my mind. It was about two unlovable characters named A and B, one obviously a hustler and the other a wimp.

The lecturer was attempting to capsulize the development of the political process, which he divided into three stages. The first stage began when A picked up a club and bashed B over the head; B, when he had recovered, was more than willing to do whatever A wanted him to do. The second stage was when A put on a Halloween mask and scared the devil out of B; B again was willing to do whatever A wanted him to do. The professor regarded the second stage as an improvement over the first, but he reserved his finest ecstasies for the third stage, in which A did so many favors for B that the latter was willing to do anything, within reason, that A wanted done. As far as he was concerned, that was the process of civilized politics.

In a very real sense, it can be said that the Irish in the United States began with the third stage. Of course, they might have had to bludgeon their way into a position from which they could dispense favors—assuming that big cities made policemen of them in order to convert them from gangsters into useful citizens. But they used control of the police forces and the fire departments as a means of gaining capital for trading purposes. They went quickly

[59]

to stage three, and used control of the protective mechanisms as an instrument for serving larger ends.

Government by doing favors was not invented by the Irish immigrants. It was a method that sprang up as soon as people at the lower end of the social scale were brought into the political equation. It was Andrew Jackson who, when he became President, laid down the principle that "to the victor belong the spoils." Government by "gentlemen"—which was the way in which the United States began—can operate without using the formal instruments of patronage. But when ordinary citizens start to move into positions of power, they see no reason why they should forgo any of the direct economic benefits.

Actually, however, the resemblance between the machine politics built by the Irish and my professor's third stage in the political process was not squarely on the mark. In the first place, the age of Jackson was one of intense ideological activity. His Democrats wanted power in order to pass laws involving homesteading, tariffs, territorial expansion, and encouragement of low interest rates. The jobs that were passed out were merely rewards for supporting the "right cause"—a means to an end and not the end itself.

Second, there was a psychological approach by the Irish machines that must be taken into account. They did not merely "do favors." If that had been the outer limits of their techniques, they would not have lasted very long. In the real world, we never like people who do things for us because that gives them a chance to demonstrate their superiority. We much prefer the people for whom we can do favors because they give us a chance to demonstrate *our* superiority. Our truly healthful relationships are those in which we *exchange* helpful acts, thus leaving all involved a means of preserving their dignity. This was the true method of the Irish machine and it was a method elevated into a ruling principle of government. The ultimate goal of political activity was to perform social services as compensation for the support of the people who were making their living as a result of those services.

The dispensation of patronage by the Irish bosses was only a part of their operation. Most of the jobs passed out directly by

City Hall went to members of the machine, who could be depended upon to keep organizational interests in mind as they discharged their official obligations. This meant special attention to such city offices as public works, regulation of weights and measures, business zoning permits, parade permits, and other regulatory functions that held a high degree of control over the social and economic life of the city. Such control opened up channels through which unregistered sums of money could flow into the pockets of "deserving" political leaders. It also opened up channels through which favors could be performed for nonmachine citizens, who would be likely to "vote right" in return.

These favors hit at every level. Manufacturing industries located in areas of intense pilferage could receive extra and intensive police protection if they knew how to dispense campaign funds. Small storekeepers who had marked the proper slots on the ballot could negotiate for special loading and unloading permits with the traffic departments. Construction companies who understood how to deal with the "organization" found their legal difficulties to be resolved very quickly. Men and women who needed temporary jobs in a hurry found that a letter from a ward leader would put them on a payroll, and they did not even have to know the leader—they could negotiate the deal through their precinct or block captain.

In Chicago, for example, one of the more visible sources of summer employment was Riverview Park. But most of the available jobs—as I learned one summer during my college days when I had to get on a payroll somehow—were open only upon the written endorsement of a ward leader. It had been many years since I had lived on the near East Side, and my father had left Chicago. He still knew people, however, and the necessary letter came through. I was taken on as a "shill," assigned to a wheel where I pretended to win a large amount of money every fifteen or twenty minutes. The park, dependent upon all sorts of licenses and permits, was only too happy to turn over its personnel practices to the officials who could decide whether such things could be issued or denied.

Of course, there were many other favors that could be performed once political control had been established. Local judges could be lenient toward those who had endorsements from the proper quarters. Special consideration could be available for the "right" patients in the County Hospital. Eviction notices could be lost for tenants who were on the right side of the political spectrum, and landlords in low-rent districts would not be too quick to evict anyway on a word from a precinct captain. (Of course, ignoring the word would guarantee the landlord problems with garbage collection and all sorts of nitpicking city ordinances of which he had never heard.)

The elevation of patronage in exchange for votes as an ultimate political principle has been the major factor in criticism of the Irish machines. To reformers, the lack of ideology was absolutely infuriating and to intellectuals it was the subject of scorn—even among Irish intellectuals. The views of the latter were very well summed up by Daniel Patrick Moynihan in 1963 when he produced an essay entitled "The Irish" (in a book called *Beyond the Melting Pot*). The machines, he said, "did not know what to do with power once they got it. They never thought of politics as an instrument of social change." That meant that those who *were* interested in social change looked upon the Celtic ward bosses and precinct captains as "the enemy."

In terms of American literature, the machines took a heavy beating from muckraking writers in the late nineteenth and early twentieth century. It was not until they had become relics of the past that a few kindly words for them were put down on paper. The first important work of popular fiction to take an understanding look at the Irish bosses was *The Last Hurrah* by Edwin O'Connor, published in 1956. It may still be the best source for shedding light on the whole question. The protagonist—a thinly disguised James Michael Curley—was Frank Skeffington, whose career is traced from a poor boy with no opportunities whatsoever to mayor of Boston, where he could, and did, open opportunities for others. The novel made Curley one of the best-known of all Irish American politicians.

The critics, however, never found a satisfactory explanation for a salient point—the ability of the Irish machines to win elections. Stuffed ballot boxes and the votes that could be traced back to names on the tombstones couldn't explain everything. To stuff those ballot boxes and get away with it, the bosses had to have solid support from the populace. In a democracy, the seizure of power does not rest upon possession of guns and bayonets. Irish rule of the big cities was at least accepted by a majority of the inhabitants who did not feel strongly enough about the tilting of the election process to do anything about it.

The basic truth was that the machines fulfilled a need of American development. The transition from an agricultural and trading economy had produced conditions of instability. A manufacturing economy jumbles people together and forces a type of interaction that can become violent. Italians, Jews, Poles, Germans could easily have created violent warring camps. Furthermore, the formal structure of the American divided-powers form of government can lead to stalemate. The Irish organizations became a unifying factor in our major cities, as well as a means of distributing economic rewards among immigrants in ways that alleviated desperation and eased their entry into an alien society.

There had been some sporadic political moves by Irish residents of New York City as early as 1817. New York, the largest urban area in the nation, probably also had the largest Irish population. It also had a political organization named Tammany Hall, already corrupt, and Celtic eyes spotted its possibilities almost at once. But in that period, there simply were not enough Irish-Americans looking for a dinner to change the direction of New York politics. The early Irish politicians differed little, if at all, from the nativist elements already in the country.

In time the population question was resolved. In 1845, 2 percent of Boston's population was Irish. By 1855, that figure had grown to 20 percent. By 1850, the Irish-born population of New York was 26 percent, and that figure rose to about 33 percent if second and third generations are included. The high point of Irish immigration came in 1851 when 218,000 entered the United

States. That figure is probably an underestimate, since no one can be sure how many went to Canada first and then simply crossed the border.

The influx was not confined to the port cities. The refugees from the Potato Famine found a country that was beginning to discover itself. Railroads were starting to span the continent, and the canals and rivers had become major arteries for interstate commerce. Both supplied plenty of jobs for musclemen who were willing to work cheap. This resulted in a further migration to the interior—not to the farms but to Albany, Buffalo, Cleveland, Chicago, Peoria, and Omaha. In the 1850s there was another move —this time to California because of the Gold Rush. From San Francisco, the Irish fanned out to Denver, Virginia City, and Butte, Montana. In my active years as a political aide, the Irish character of Butte was regarded as an important factor in the campaign plans of Montana politicians.

Those who went West engaged in militant labor unionism as well as politics. The Pennsylvania coal fields produced the Molly Maguires (named after antilandlord organizations in Ireland), and the metal mines of the Rocky Mountain states became the foundation for the Western Federation of Miners (later to be converted into the famed Industrial Workers of the World, or the IWW). As for the Knights of Labor, a secret union, it was dominated by the Irish when it reached its peak in the 1880s. None of these organizations, incidentally, was very strong on ideology. A halfhearted attempt was made to imbue the IWW with the revolutionary syndicalist theories of Georges Sorel, but it came to very little. There were many members of the IWW (known as Wobblies) who were willing to toss a stick of dynamite at an employer, but it was a gesture of rage with no coherent philosophy behind it.

Militant unionism, however, was not the dominant drive of the American Irish; it was only one aspect of Celtic character, which today finds expression in the Provisional IRA and other terrorist groups fighting in Ulster. The mainstream of Gaelic culture was in persuasion and political maneuver. Even the Irish reputation for brawling is something of a myth. It started because the

Irish were still in the slums when boxing first became popular on a large scale in this country. But the boxers were not boxers because they were Irish. They were boxers, because it was a way to make a quick buck—just as it is for blacks and Hispanics, who dominate the prize rings today. The slums breed tough people.

The Irish who were to shape the future were busily at work taking over other instruments of social control. From controlling the police and the fire departments, they went on to the conservative construction trades unions, which they dominated by 1890, and the mass-transportation systems of major cities such as New York, which they ran into the 1960s. Finally came the political organizations that were already here—the branches of the Democratic Party and Tammany Hall itself.

As it has in so many other aspects, New York City led the way in forming the Irish political machines. The Irish captured Tammany Hall and held on to it up into the mid-twentieth century, when both Tammany and machine politics ceased to be effective. The last Tammany boss to make any impact upon the public consciousness was Carmine De Sapio—hardly an Irish name but hardly a successful boss either.

It is interesting that the first of the great Tammany chieftains was not Irish but Scots. He was William Marcy Tweed, a descendant of blacksmiths who plied their trade along the banks of the Tweed River, the eastern border with England. By the age of twenty-five he had joined one of the Irish firefighting companies, and that became his springboard into Tammany and into politics. In a very few years, he was conspiring with such men as Peter "Brains" Sweeny and Richard "Slippery Dick" Connolly, to oust Mayor Fernando Wood from Tammany Hall. The effort was successful, and by 1859 Tweed had complete control of the organization. He knew what he wanted to do with it: Make money. In terms of greed, Tweed was one of the greatest of the bosses. Connable and Silberfarb quote him in their book *The History of Tammany Hall* as dismissing the candidacy for reelection of City Comptroller Matthew Brennan because "You won't make money yourself, nor let others make any. . . ."

Tweed was not averse to making money for himself or for those who helped him make it. The power he amassed through the Irish machine seems incredible in retrospect. He controlled Tammany, City Hall, the state legislature, two-thirds of the New York Supreme Court, and the governor's mansion in Albany. Such power, when applied to the business of making money, could produce results. Tweed and his cohorts milked the city treasury of hundreds of thousands of dollars. In the county courthouse, erected under Tweed direction, each cuspidor cost $190, and the bill for thermometers came to $7,500. The original cost estimates had been $250,000 but the final bill was $12.5 million—which is somewhat astounding even to a modern generation accustomed to cost overruns on Defense Department contracts. Furthermore, Tweed used his position to acquire stock in the Erie Railroad, whose income from both operations and stock sales simply vanished. How much Tweed and his friends made on that one will never be known with any certainty.

Whom the gods would destroy they first make mad, and Tweed was an excellent example. He became the target of every liberal reformer in the nation and inspired the famous Nast cartoons. In 1871 he lost control of both the New York City delegation to the state legislature and the City Council, and a series of very embarrassing investigations were set underway. Finally, he was arrested on 104 counts of bribery and malfeasance and sentenced to twelve years' imprisonment. The sentence was reduced to a fine, and he was rearrested as part of a civil suit to recover the monies he had stolen. Released to visit his family, he made a bolt for Europe but was taken into custody by Spanish authorities and returned to the United States. He died at the age of fifty-five.

One would think that Tammany would die with Tweed, who, for all practical purposes, had been the organization for well over a decade. His corruption was Tammany corruption, and the two could not be told apart. However, there was a leader waiting in the wings who was of a far different stripe. It was "Honest John" Kelly—a man who had earned the nickname because it fit his character. He was a deeply religious man, shot through with a piety so pronounced that he made many people around him uncomfortable. Like Tweed, he started out in a volunteer fire company, which led him into Tammany and eventually to a seat in the House of Representatives. But unlike Tweed, he became a sincere member of the reform wing of Tammany Hall. Despite his reformist tendencies, he was strong with Irish voters, because he was the only Catholic in the House of Representatives and engaged in almost daily verbal battles with the anti-Catholic Know-Nothings.

It was probably desperation that forced Tammany to turn to Kelly. But he demonstrated immediately that he was a man who knew how to use power for something other than adding to his income. There was a quick reorganization, in which the remnants of the Tweed Ring were ousted and replaced not only by Irish pols but by what we call today "solid citizens" such as Horatio Seymour and August Belmont. Kelly's goal was to convert Tammany into an organization that performed social services for people in the lower depths—and he succeeded. Kelly was the first Irish Catholic to take over the top post, and what Tammany became in the last part of the nineteenth and the first part of the twentieth centuries was almost entirely his doing. There were still plenty of Tammany men who missed no chance to line their pockets. But they worked for the privilege by helping the people that needed help. Typical of the kind of men who followed Kelly was George Washington Plunkitt.

Plunkitt, in his diary, presented what has become the classic description of the activities of Tammany leaders in the post-Kelly era. A day in his life is worth quoting in full:

> 2 A.M. Awakened by a boy with message from a bartender to bail him out of jail. 3 A.M. Back to bed. 6 A.M. Fire engines, up and off to the scene to see my election district captains tending the burnt-out tenants. Got names for new homes. 8:30 to police court. Six drunken constituents on hand. Got four released by a timely word to the judge. Paid the others' fines. Nine

o'clock to Municipal court. Told an election district captain to act as lawyer for a widow threatened with dispossession. 11 to 3 P.M. Found jobs for four constituents . . .

The rest of the day was spent in attendance at Italian and Jewish funerals, a meeting of district captains, a church fair, a session in the clubhouse with pushcart peddlers, and a Jewish wedding. At midnight he got to bed.

It must be understood that Plunkitt was not averse to making money out of his job. His only rule was that it be within the boundaries of what he termed "honest graft"—meaning that he felt he was entitled to his cut in performing services for the people.

"The politician who steals is worse than a thief," Plunkitt said. "He is a fool. With the grand opportunities all around for the man with a political pull, there's no excuse for stealing a cent."

Obviously, Plunkitt, like almost every other human being, tended to see his conduct in a favorable light. It is part of human nature to compose laudatory press releases about ourselves when we have a chance of "going public." What makes Plunkitt's words noteworthy, however, is that a similar picture of the activities of a typical ward boss was drawn by an implacable foe of machine politics—the famous social service worker Jane Addams. It did not take her very long after she founded Hull House in Chicago (1889) to learn that one of her principal problems was Johnny Powers, an alderman and boss of the 19th Ward.

The ward was virtually made to order for an Irish machine. It was made up largely of immigrants and their first generation descendants from Ireland, Bohemia, Poland, Italy, and Russia, the latter mostly Jews. Like Plunkitt, Powers had seen his opportunities and taken advantage of them. He was chairman of the Chicago City Council Finance Committee and headed the caucus that distributed the chairmanships on the other committees. In addition, he was chairman of the Cook County Democratic Committee— which in the Chicago of those days was tantamount to city government. These positions were in charge of the distribution of street railway franchises and rights-of-way for laying cables and telephone lines. This gave him virtual control of the hiring of streetcar employees and telephone operators—a disproportionate number of whom came from the 19th Ward and were eager to vote for Johnny Powers as many times as he wished. He also had floating funds with which to pay rent for the penniless, finance funerals, and help the sick get into County Hospital.

It was inevitable that Johnny Powers and Jane Addams—both strong-minded people regardless of their other characteristics—would clash. She thought in terms of education and opening up opportunities that would give the residents of the ward a path out of the slums. He thought in terms of keeping the residents where they were: If he doled out enough jobs and favors to make them reasonably content with their lot, they would be reluctant to move to other areas, where they could not depend upon his protection against an alien world. Addams also thought of services such as garbage collection in terms of civic health and launched campaigns to make the process more efficient. He thought of such services in terms of patronage and had no intention of permitting the establishment of a merit system that might weaken his authority to distribute jobs as he saw fit.

She did manage to win on the garbage collection by having herself appointed a garbage inspector (it is not clear how she outflanked Johnny Powers on this one) and literally taking to the streets at 6 A.M. to check on collections. She was able to raise such a storm that the garbage situation did improve. But most of her early battles were lost. They did succeed in convincing her that the struggle could be won only through political means, and she mounted a number of campaigns to oust the ward boss from his political control. She won some, lost some. But in the process, she grew in knowledge—coming up with one of the most perceptive understandings of machine politics ever produced by a reformer. In 1898, she wrote a paper for the *International Journal of Ethics* (see appendix), which reviewed what Powers had done to keep the people in the ward in jobs and contrasted his activities with those of the reformers seeking clean government. She said:

"The sense of just dealing comes apparently much later than the desire for protection and kindness. The Alderman is really elected because he is a good friend and neighbor."

Most prescient of her observations concerned a "better element" speaker she had brought into the ward in opposition to Powers. He was a complete flop:

> He certainly succeeded in irrevocably injuring the chances of the candidate for whom he was speaking. The speaker's standard of ethics was upright dealing in positions of public trust. The standard of ethics held by his audience was, being good to the poor and speaking gently of the dead [he had attacked an earlier ward leader of the Powers variety]. If he considered them corrupt and illiterate voters, they quite honestly held him a blackguard.

To keep the record clear, it should be stated at this point that the experience did not convert Jane Addams to active participation in machine politics. But it did give her a sense of those things that had to be done if the reformers were to prevail. Her final words summed up a philosophy that other "honest government" advocates should have heeded:

> If we discover that men of low ideals and corrupt practice are forming popular political standards simply because such men stand by and for and with the people, then nothing remains but to obtain a like sense of identification before we can hope to modify ethical standards.

One wonders from both Plunkitt's and Jane Addams' testimony whether Honest John Kelly is so little known today because he lived up to his name.

Although Kelly probably had more to do with the powerful machine that Tammany became, he is strangely enough the least known of the great leaders—possibly because he did not embrace Plunkitt's theories of graft. He was followed by much better known men—such as Croker and Murphy, whose names come automatically to the fore when one goes into the history of New York City politics. Even Jimmy Walker—a rather inconsequential mayor in the 1920s—receives more recognition. At this point, however, it is time to leave Tammany for a temporary spell. To understand the development of the Irish political machines, it is essential to take a close look at other cities where they followed different paths.

Chapter 7

♣

The NUTS and BOLTS

THE MACHINES DIFFERED FROM CITY TO CITY, BUT A COMMON denominator is that the leaders were gregarious men. In every city they plunged early into work or social activities—mostly some version of salesmanship—that kept them in contact with other people. Quite often, this meant running a saloon as did Christopher A. "Blind Boss" Buckley in San Francisco and James Pendergast —father of Thomas J., Harry Truman's ally—who founded a political dynasty in Kansas City in the 1890s. Even today, when the saloon has been largely replaced by the cocktail lounge, a drinking spot is a marvelous location for taking the pulse of the public, for exchanging confidences and forming close ties. In the nineteenth century, the saloon was something of a "club" staffed by bartenders who acquired social followings. It was not very difficult to translate this into political followings. There are some theories that the saloons were the real backbone of the political machines. I know of no way to prove it, but I tend to believe it because my father told me so.

John F. "Honey Fitz" Fitzgerald took a different route. Although his Irish-born father had a combination grocery *and* liquor store in the North End of Boston, he established himself as a fire insurance salesman, a position that brought him into intimate contact with homeowners and influential businessmen. He used his commercial contacts deliberately to build ward power. He joined every association and club, and kept careful track of everyone in his district who needed a job. He was adept at matching workers with opportunities—an art that reached a high state of development I witnessed personally many years later in Chicago under the Kelly-Nash machine.

For James Michael Curley, the springboard to political power

[75]

in 1890s Boston was the operation of a horse-cart delivery route for a grocer. It took him all through the city, and at every stop he exercised his considerable charm to impress his personality upon the customers. In the nineteenth century, livery stables and cigar stores (the kind that placed a wooden statue of an Indian at the front door) were social hangouts, and Curley became familiar with all of them. In New York City, the route into politics led through the associations formed to support volunteer fire companies—a path taken by Tweed, Kelly, Smith, and others.

The Irish gained power rapidly throughout the second half of the nineteenth century, largely through strength among policemen and firemen. But power must be harnessed and concentrated in order to achieve conscious shaping of a society. Focusing their power was the role of the early bosses. They appreciated the leverage that was growing out of the protective services of society, and they had definite ideas of how to translate it into economic and political strength.

In Boston, where in the 1890s one third of the voters were Irish, about all the boss had to do was to secure agreement among his colleagues and he would gain control. Since he was dealing with a people accustomed to informal methods of cooperation, this was not difficult. However, there were not many cities like Boston. In most areas, the Irish leaders had to display a high degree of political skill in order to establish hegemony. As a general rule, the tactic was to find "leverage" positions. This can best be explained by an apocryphal example.

Let us return to our fictitious Officer O'Malley. After his pleasant greeting to Giovanelli, think of him continuing on his beat past a speakeasy, where some illegal booze is being sold, past a floating crap game in a park, past a sidewalk table where knickknacks are on sale by an unlicensed salesman. O'Malley is a good cop, and he is not going to turn a blind eye to violent crime or anything he considers "immoral"—such as peddling pornography. But he will be remarkably understanding when the only offense is ignoring nitpicking rules that make life so intolerable in big cities when they are imposed to the nth degree. The popularity of the

Irish cop was that he knew when laws should *not* be enforced. And when he was teamed with a precinct captain or a ward leader, he became one of the most potent political instruments ever devised in a democracy.

Of course, O'Malley—as well as Kelly, Guilfoyle, O'Halloran, and O'Boyle—was only one step on the road to power. It was an important step, because it was a means of gaining votes—extralegal but not glaring enough to cause serious trouble. The minor misdemeanors O'Malley ignored, when put together, could add up to some tremendous gaps in law enforcement. But individually they would not overly excite any crusader for clean government. At the same time, however, the rewards to the machine politicians of such activities were not very high. Generally speaking, they were a method of getting into governmental positions where the rewards could be high—both financially and politically.

A major benefit of political office was control of the city's public works agencies. This meant kickbacks to the appropriate officials, jobs for deserving Democrats and cooperative unions and civic organizations. There were lush rewards in the street paving, sewage, and electricity departments. In Chicago, one of the most notorious examples in the 1920s was the building, at a cost of $1 million, of a bridle path alongside the sewage canal where there was little probability that equestrians would be attracted.

There could be little doubt that many politicians lined their pockets in such a manner. In New York, George Washington Plunkitt, the Tammany boss, boasted openly to journalists that he had cleaned up considerable cash when he got an advance tip on a new park that was going to be built. He quickly bought up some land before the plan became known and sold it at premium prices. He saw nothing wrong with the transaction. "It's just like looking ahead in Wall Street or in the coffee or cotton market," he explained.

The informal understandings with industry, however, had objectives additional to the accumulation of wealth. The most important was control over types of additional patronage. Huge mass industries, such as the big meat packers in Chicago, were quite amenable to using clearance from ward leaders and precinct captains when they had to hire in a hurry. As far as they were concerned, it was a form of insurance. Everybody was happy. The hiring cost the managers of the stockyards nothing (the owners may have known nothing about it, the practice being in the hands of hiring bosses); the workers got on a badly needed payroll; and the ward leaders basked in the gratitude of the workers.

Moreover, the bosses were able to offer their favors with an air of ease and warmth that contrasted sharply with the sterile impersonality of social service agencies. People in trouble were not asked to fill out long forms, to explain the presence in their house of an unaccountable man or woman, to list the steps they had taken to conserve fuel bills, to attend lectures on economical nutrition and birth control. All that was involved was a handshake and a friendly smile. It was not charity but a dignified exchange —a job for a vote.

Furthermore, the political boss went out of his way to share the joys and the sorrows of his people. To their immigrant constituencies, the most important part of their world centered around the church or the synagogue—the key to baptisms, marriage, Bar Mitzvahs, and funerals. The ward leaders, precinct captains, and block wardens kept careful track of all such events and inserted themselves into every ceremony as a friend. There would be small gifts for baptisms, Bar Mitzvahs, and commencements, and attendance at weddings where afterwards the ward leader would dance with the bride and throw money in the hat. There would also be help with the funerals—even to the extent of bearing all the costs when the people were too poor. Jane Addams noted:

> The Alderman saves the very poorest of his constituents from that awful horror of burial by the county; he provides carriages for the poor, who otherwise could not have them; for the more prosperous he sends extra carriages, so that they might invite more friends . . . It may be too much to say that all the relatives and friends who ride in the carriages provided by the Alderman's

bounty vote for him but they are certainly influenced by his kindness, and talk of his virtues during the long hours of the ride back and forth from the suburban cemetery. A man who would ask at such a time where all this money comes from would be considered sinister.

One senses a feeling of wonderment in Jane Addams as her sight—unusually clear for a reformer—began to take in the realities of the machine. She asks herself where the money comes from and concludes that it was raised from the sums gouged out of industry by the machines. Thus, for example, street railways had to pay for the privilege of getting franchises in plain, cold cash, as well as supplying the boss with jobs he could distribute. The companies could do so only by raising the streetcar fares, which meant that the people who were getting the favors were also financing them. Even a clear exposition of what was happening would make no difference.

> The more primitive people accept the truthful statement of its sources [the Alderman's slush funds] without any shock to their moral sense [Jane Addams wrote]. To their simple minds, he gets it "from the rich" and so long as he again gives it out to the poor, as a true Robin Hood, with open hand, they have no objections to offer.

Whatever else one may wish to say about Jane Addams, she certainly understood the political machine and might have been more successful in bringing about its downfall had others who shared her goals also shared her acumen. As it was, her success with Hull House becomes explainable when one reads her analysis of how things worked in the 19th Ward. She had learned—the hard way—how to deal with human beings out of a different culture.

The basic point that should be borne in mind is that power bred more power, which in turn bred even more power. The ability to deliver votes led to the election of the machine candidates to mayoralties and city councils. That, in turn, led to appointments over regulatory bodies, which in turn resulted in a willingness of industry and other wealth-generating organizations to cooperate with the bosses, and that, in turn, opened up new possibilities of patronage and money. The circle went round and round always spiraling upward. In the 1920s, everyone thought it was a permanent way of life. It was realized that other ethnic groups were coming to the fore, but it was assumed that this would merely change the names of the players. After all, there was no real reason why Czechs, Poles, Italians, and Hungarians should not learn from the experiences of the Irish. As a matter of fact, they did.

The bottom line, however, was getting votes. Many of the Irish pols became arrogant and developed extensive cases of hubris. But even they realized that everything would collapse if the votes did not come through. With so much at stake, it is little wonder that they sought some extra insurance in the form of delivering majorities at the polls whether or not they really existed.

The Irish machines did not actually invent ballot-box stuffing. It was just as prevalent in Texas as it was in Chicago or New York. But they did invent the techniques used in the large cities, and this is worthy of passing comment. There were three essential elements to the operation. The first consisted of registered lists of voters who would not show up at the polls and become obstreperous when they discovered that their votes had already been cast. The second was control over the officials who were appointed to supervise voting procedures in every precinct. The third was a corps of live human beings who were not overly particular about *where* they voted, *how often* they voted, or *under what name* they voted.

The first two elements required only control over crucial city machinery. Interestingly enough, this included the bureaus of vital statistics. There would be some real problems if the poll lists were genuinely pruned when people died or if research into birth certificates cast doubt upon the bona fides of certain registrants. The third element, in a sense, was the easiest to handle. The nation harbored many hoboes, tramps, and footloose bums who, with the exception of hoboes (hoboes would work—they just wouldn't stay in one place very long), didn't like work but were quite willing to pick up some loose change.

Of course, throughout much of the nineteenth century, the step of finding "eligible" voters could be forgotten altogether. All that was necessary was an ample supply of printed ballots and of poll watchers who knew when to take their eyes off the boxes. But as voter registration became increasingly prevalent and increasingly efficient, ballot-box stuffing became too raw. Voting "floaters" and "drifters" cost more money, but the stakes were high enough to justify the needed investment. The machines always managed to stay one step ahead of reformers.

In Chicago, the art was brought to its highest point by "Bathhouse (pronounced Bat-house) John" Coughlin and "Hinky-Dink" Kenna in the famous (or infamous—take your pick) 1st Ward. This was an area of brothels, saloons, strip-tease joints, and flophouses. For weeks before an election, agents of the duo would scour the Midwest for every tramp and bum they could find. They would house them in the flophouses on South State Street with a huge vat of alcohol in the middle of the floor to hold them there. On election day they would be driven to eighteen or twenty precincts to cast a ballot—for which they would be rewarded with 50 cents—in each one. The names on the poll registration lists were taken off tombstones. After all, the franchise was so highly valued by the Irish that they did not believe death was a serious disqualification. It was a process widely known in Chicago, and the *Tribune*—which tended to be a reformist Republican paper— would occasionally write sarcastic articles about it. But nothing much was done to put an end the practice of voting floaters, and the only Republican mayor elected in the 1920s was Big Bill Thompson, who carried on a personal feud with the newspaper that overrode all other considerations.

The 1930s and 1940s put something of a crimp in the practice, because of the rise of new types of labor organizations that were less amenable to pacts with the bosses than the older construction trades. Primarily, these were the industrial unions set up by the

CIO. They were vulnerable to communist infiltration, but they were led by such politically sophisticated men as Walter Reuther (the United Automobile Workers), Sidney Hillman (Amalgamated Clothing Workers), Dave Dubinsky (International Ladies Garment Workers), Alex Rose (Hat, Cap, and Millinery Workers), and others who knew how to handle the machines and often wound up supplanting them altogether.

The kind of power that was massed by machine politics obviously opened up delightful prospects of wealth—especially delightful to men whose ancestors had come to the United States looking for a square meal. It is not at all surprising that many of them succumbed to temptation. They had emerged from the dog-eat-dog society that always develops in slums, and they had managed to acquire some leverage over the business world whose turn-of-the century members were distinctly piratical in their operations. Plunkitt's observation comparing his land deal to "looking ahead" in Wall Street was not without point. Big businessmen weren't called Robber Barons for nothing.

No one will ever be certain, however, just how much "boodlery" was involved in the machine operations. Most of the leaders realized early that it was dangerous—and foolish—to pocket public funds outright. Again, Plunkitt is invaluable.

"I've told you how I got rich by honest graft," he said to an inquirer. "Now, let me tell you that most politicians who are accused of robbin' the city get rich the same way. They didn't steal a dollar from the city treasury. They just seen their opportunities and took them. That is why, when a reform administration comes in and spends a half million dollars in tryin' to find the public robberies they talked about in the campaign, they don't find them.

"The books are always all right. The money in the city treasury is all right. Everything is all right. All they can show is that the Tammany heads of department looked after their friends, within the law, and gave them what opportunities they could to make honest graft. Now let me tell you that's never goin' to hurt Tammany with the people."

In the last quarter of the twentieth century, there are very few people who are going to agree with Plunkitt. But his words are worth studying, because they illustrate the problem of quantifying the amount of graft that actually existed. In most cases, the machine leaders insisted on fairly careful bookkeeping. An examination would turn up many instances of exorbitant spending. But who is to say that the money was being dispensed crudely to wind up in the pockets of organization leaders, passed out because of poor judgment, or simply because of special circumstances? Furthermore, there were too many unquestionably honest men associated with machine politics—Kelly and Al Smith, for example—to indict the whole organizations.

What insights into the system are possible come through the careers of machine politicians who were possessed of inordinate greed. The most notorious, of course, was Tweed.

In comparison to him, every other known instance of boodlery seems to be small potatoes. For example, a state legislative committee (Case-McAllister) investigated Boss Hague of Jersey City in 1928 and 1929. What it found were such things as the following: collections from movie-theater owners for nonenforcement of the Sunday closing law in Jersey City (between $50,000 and $60,000 a year); favoritism for a Hague friend, who received a contract for building a bridge; indications, but little direct evidence, of "protection" for illegal horse-betting parlors; and padded city payrolls. Generally speaking, these were sums that would have been swept off the table among Tweed's people. Hague, on Constitutional grounds, refused to answer questions on sums of money he had allegedly received from local businessmen. There was little the committee could do other than to report the facts. Obviously, the public did not care very much, and Hague remained in power until he retired voluntarily in 1947.

Thomas J. Pendergast was another example of a political boss who got into trouble through graft—graft of the Plunkitt variety. He owned what was called the Ready-Mixed Concrete Company in Kansas City, which received an amazingly large number of contracts for city and state construction projects. He was among the first of the machine leaders to support Roosevelt in 1932, and for a number of years, his position looked invulnerable. However, an intraparty fight in Missouri turned up examples of ballot-box stuffing. Roosevelt, who thought he had become a loser, refused to help him, and he was indicted for income tax evasion in 1939 and sentenced to fifteen months in Federal prison.

In retrospect, the graft and thievery that took place in the age of the city machines is dull—except for Tweed, who was so grandiose that he was bound to attract attention. Generally speaking, it was sordid and petty, and no one can admire the men who did such things. In actual terms of damage done to the nation, however, it does not loom nearly as large a threat to us as the current savings-and-loans bailout. It is not nearly as impressive as the cost overruns that accompany so many Pentagon weapons projects. It must be noted in any effort to discern the influence of the Irish machines on our politics and it should not be minimized. But it must be taken as only one part of the story.

Chapter 8

♣

The SPREADING POWER

THE LOGICAL STARTING POINT FOR A DISCUSSION OF IRISH POLITical machines is New York City. There is probably no other location where Celtic control was so complete and, in addition, no other place where power was so centralized. In Manhattan, the vehicle was Tammany Hall, which, after the collapse of the Tweed Ring, was dominated by such stalwart Hibernians as Honest John Kelly, Richard Croker, and Charles F. Murphy. From 1874 up to the pre–World War I era, those three men exercised—in turn— virtually an autocracy over the nation's largest metropolis.

Tammany was founded in 1789 as a patriotic organization opposed to centralization of the United States government. The name came from a semilegendary—possibly altogether legendary—Indian chief of the Delaware Nation who supposedly inhabited the area of Princeton University. In mythology, he was wise and benevolent, and prior to the American Revolution, his name was used by Republican organizations. During the formative days of the Republic, it was tied closely to national, as well as local, government. The officers of the society were given Indian titles, and the rank of Great Grand Sachem was bestowed upon the President of the United States through the administration of John Quincy Adams and Andrew Jackson. The members were widely known as sympathizers of the French revolutionaries and followers of the philosophy of Thomas Jefferson.

Against that background, it seems incongruous that an organization of such character would become the major vehicle for a patronage dispensing city machine. But that is exactly what happened. New York was the most rapidly growing city in the nation, and by the 1840s, Tammany was devoting most of its activities to local affairs. It was pro-Democratic and anti-Whig

[87]

and a natural target for infiltration by elements in our society who were at odds with the older "respectable" establishment. When the New York Irish began to probe the opportunities for political activity, it offered the most obvious path to power.

By 1868, when the organization built a new headquarters, Tammany was completely under the control of William M. Tweed—a Scotsman whose two top lieutenants were named Peter B. Sweeny and Richard B. Connolly. The organization was so powerful that its endorsement was generally equivalent to Democratic nomination and to election for city offices. It was also, however, greedy, and the Tweed ring went down in history as the most notorious example of corruption in American politics.

The collapse of the ring should have been the end of Tammany but it was taken over by a remarkable leader—Honest John Kelly—who succeeded in bringing the graft within "reasonable" limits. He was followed by men like Croker and Murphy, who may not have been as rigidly honest but who were too astute to allow their organization to wind up in the widescale public looting that had characterized Tweed.

The first forays out of New York machine politics were in neighboring New Jersey and Connecticut, where factories hungry for cheap labor sprang up. However, that was not the limit of the spread. One of the features of the second half of the nineteenth century was the development of mass transportation, not only in the cities but between the cities as well. Boats proceeding up the Hudson River carried Irish crews to do the dirty work. It was only a matter of time until what many regard as the most efficient, though not most spectacular, of all Celtic organizations—the O'Connells—was established in Albany. The Erie Canal brought the Irish to Buffalo, and the railroads brought them to Chicago and Peoria. Many of them made their way south and west from there.

They did not remain unskilled very long. By 1900, they had virtual control of the plumbers and the carpenters, and bricklaying was looked upon as a Celtic art. It was popularly supposed that Irishmen were constantly engaged in splitting bricks to hurl them at each other, and the half-brick came to be known as Irish confetti. Perhaps more significant, however, is the fact that by 1900, through patronage appointments, 20 percent of all Northern public schoolteachers bore Irish names, and in Chicago—the terminal point of so many railroads—the figure was one third. Add to this the police and firefighting forces, and what emerges is the common base for all the machines—securing control over basic necessities of life.

The methods used by the machines varied from city to city, and there was very little else in the way of common denominators other than that mentioned in the previous paragraph. In New York, the organization tended to one-man boss rule. But in Boston, the leaders split into independent dukedoms, which battled with each other sufficiently to permit the occasional election of a reform administration. In cities such as St. Louis, where the Irish population was not very large, they tended to concentrate on keeping other factions divided so they could come through the center. Whatever the method, however, they had the political savvy to find some means of manipulating the available forces.

To most Americans, the ultimate Irish city is Boston, even more than Dublin. The reputation is merited. Boston is one of the closest United States ports to Europe (and therefore passage was by relatively low fare), and it was also convenient for those who had reached the New World by way of Montreal to stop and settle down. Consequently, Boston, the home of the most staid of the Protestant, New England aristocrats, suddenly found itself at the receiving end of a double stream of Celts. It became a divided city, in which an anti-Romish elite stared uncomfortably—and perhaps with a tinge of fear—at a seething mass of what the old-time Yankees regarded as Catholic barbarians. There was reason for their apprehensions. From 1850 to 1855, the number of naturalized (mostly Irish) voters in Suffolk County rose by 300 percent whereas the native-born vote only rose by 14 percent. Furthermore, some Irish had been there long enough to account for part of the native increase.

Today, in character Boston is an Irish enclave. What most

Americans think of as an Irish accent is actually a Boston accent with Irish overtones, and only on Beacon Hill or in the Union League club does one find the Boston of the Adamses, the Lodges, Louisa May Alcott, Oliver Wendell Holmes, or Ralph Waldo Emerson. In history, it was the Yankee Hub of the Universe. But in the public consciousness today, Boston is the stronghold of Jack, Bobby, and Ted Kennedy, of James Michael Curley, of David I. Walsh, of John W. McCormack, and of "Tip" O'Neill.

This may be due to the efforts of Boston Irish to publicize themselves as "the Irish" with the same tactics that Texans use to advertise themselves as Texans. A casual stroll through the streets will reveal as many other nationalities as one would expect to find in any East Coast seaport. Whatever the truth about the Irish character of the city, however, it definitely produced some colorful Irish politicians. Boston also produced the first Irish Catholic President of the United States—an event that may have brought an end to the Irish as a cohesive and separate group in the United States everywhere except in Boston.

The best known of the Irish "bosses" today is probably John F. Honey Fitz Fitzgerald. He was not necessarily the strongest of the Irish leaders, but John F. Kennedy was his grandson, and any connection with a President confers a degree of immortality. There were other men that may have been stronger—Michael Doherty, Patrick Maguire, Michael M. Cunniff, Martin Lomasney, and Thomas Gargan. No one can forget James Michael Curley, regarded by most Americans as the quintessential Irish boss. It should be noted, incidentally, that all of these above leaders were notorious for fighting with each other, and there were frequent occasions in which a Yankee would wind up as a mayor simply because the Irish bosses were too divided.

No one would mistake Chicago for an Irish city, even though as an ethnic group the Irish displayed real power. Few of them, however, became very well known until the third decade of the twentieth century. They stayed in the background. None of them—Dunne, Brennan, McDonald, or Sullivan—was colorful. The first colorful citywide politician in the city did not appear until the 1920s. He was William Hale "Big Bill the Builder" Thompson, who was actually born in Boston but who was a non-Irish Protestant. He had, however, learned some of the tricks of the Irish political leaders and won many Irish votes running on a Republican ticket. His tactics centered around proclamations of unrelenting warfare against the British, and in one of his campaigns in the 1920s he promised that, if he were elected, he would take the first boat to England and "punch King George on the snoot." It was a surefire tactic, uniting all the major ethnic groups in the city. To the Irish Anglophobia was added the hatred of the Italians for the English, because of Ethiopia; the hatred of the Germans because of World War I, and the hatred of the Poles because of the Curzon Line. Furthermore, no one ever succeeded in locating the headquarters of the pro-English party, which did not seem to distribute much in the way of campaign material.

There were, of course, plenty of Irish leaders such as Pat Nash and Roger Sullivan, but they came late in the city's history and spent too much of their time fighting with each other. When Thompson finally passed from the scene, Chicago was taken over by Anton J. Cermak—a Czech who had mastered the Irish art of dividing the opposition and coming through the center. While riding with Roosevelt in Florida, he was killed by an assassin's bullet fired at the car. Ed Kelly and Pat Nash assumed control, to be followed by a string of Irish mayors culminating in Richard J. Daley—the last of the great bosses.

One interesting sidelight is that Chicago was never subjected to the violent type of aimless Irish gangsterism that plagued the Eastern seaboard cities during the years that followed the Potato Famine. Perhaps the Irish who reached Chicago before the Civil War were too well employed to form street gangs. But during the Prohibition era of the 1920s, ethnic gangs were formed in Chicago, and the Irish leaders were such men as Dion O'Banion and Myles and Klondike O'Donnell. These, however, were basically businessmen operating outside the law, and their battles with other gangs were for control of booze distribution in various areas of the city. They did not threaten nongang citizens with meaningless

[91]

rumbles. The Italians under Al Capone were the most efficient, and eventually wiped out all the Irish—as well as the Polish, Jewish, and German—mobsters.

In Kansas City, under the rule of the Pendergasts, it was quite a different story, since the Irish, although a minority, ran the city for a good part of the twentieth century. James Pendergast, who died in 1912 but passed on his control to his son, Thomas, gave the *New York Times* what may be the best description of the Irish boss attitude that ever came from a participant in the process.

"That's all there is to this boss business: friends," he said. "You can't make 'em vote for you. I never coerced anybody in my life. Whenever you see a man bulldozing anybody, he don't last long. Still, I've been called a boss. All there is to it is having friends, doing things for people, and then later they'll do things for you."

Pendergast's claim was justified, although somewhat incomplete. A careful study of the Irish political machines turns up very little in the way of strong-arm tactics outside Jersey City. What he left out, of course, was a description of the manner in which the hungrier ballot boxes were sometimes fed, and stalwart machine supporters had their pockets lined with greenbacks.

Horace Greeley's famous advice, "Go West, young man! Go West!" was heeded by the Irish—especially in the age of railroad building. In terms of color, Bathhouse John Coughlin rivaled any Irish leader in America, although on a much smaller scale. He had picked up the sobriquet by starting his career as a rubber in a Turkish bath. But he didn't stay there long. He was quick, and he had charm. He worked his way into the Democratic organization, and within a few years he and a friend, Hinky Dink Kenna, ruled Chicago's red-light district. He was big and flamboyant and was addicted to elaborate suits in shades of pink, fawn, and an occasional splash of red. Once a year he would hold the 1st Ward ball, which was attended by every pimp, prostitute, and bootlegger in the city. Of course, they were all "shaken down" for funds to finance the shindig, which was the most elaborate of the social season. To offset Bathhouse John, Hinky Dink, who owed his name to his small physical stature, was a taciturn, plainly dressed man who worked hard at staying *out* of the limelight and whose only extravagance was smoking one-dollar cigars in an era when a dollar was a lot of money. He kept his vest pockets crammed with them.

By 1900, important Irish centers had been established in San Francisco under Blind Boss Chris Buckley, in Buffalo under William F. Sheehan, in Albany under Patrick McCabe, in Brooklyn under Hugh McLaughlin. In some instances, the Irish machines operated through the Republican Party—notably in Philadelphia under James McManes, Pittsburgh under Chris Magee, and Cincinnati under George Cox. A budding Irish machine in Milwaukee was wiped out in 1860 when the leaders chartered a Lake Michigan steamer named the *Lady Elgin* for a round trip to Chicago. In a fog, it collided with another ship at night and went down with a tremendous loss of life.

The leaders in the cities could not, however, be called a network. The bosses understood each other and could hold very pleasant conversations when they met. But despite their possession of a common ancestry and a common profession, there was nothing that could be called cooperation. It did not exist even in the instance of two cities in the same state, such as New York City and Buffalo in New York or Chicago and Peoria in Illinois. It was not a question of dislike among brothers but simply a feeling that politics ended at the city limits. There was no need to reach outside for help.

The Democratic Party badge did little or nothing to bridge the gap. It had become a very loose alliance of Southern segregationists and Northern city bosses who were at odds on almost every issue. They would meet in national conventions every four years, but no one expected the Democrats to win the Presidency anyway so the conclaves were more social than anything else. There were some men who could be identified as national party "leaders" only because they were nominated for the Presidency. They included Horatio Seymour (1868), Horace Greeley (1871), Samuel J. Tilden (1872), William Jennings Bryan (1896, 1900, and 1908).

None of them could be considered "machine" politicians. They were simply the focal point of the forces that were creating party anarchy. The one Democrat who did reach the White House before Wilson—Grover Cleveland—was actually an antimachine Democrat. The Presidency simply didn't matter to the machines. They had all the resources they needed to maintain urban power and were under no compulsion to extend themselves.

As for their relations with the state governments, these were even more casual. In most areas outside the Solid South, state governments were Republican. Their organizational backbone could be found among the members of the Grand Army of the Republic (the Civil War veterans' society) or sons or grandsons of the GAR. In the cities, state legislatures were regarded as nuisances to be kept at bay. The Irish machines were parochial in the full sense of the word. They had no political principles, which meant that there was no reason for them to unite with other groups outside their bailiwick. They existed to control cities by buying votes with services. The few Irish that did approach government or society with political concepts were largely in the West and tended to be semirevolutionary in character—the Western Federation of Miners, the Knights of Labor, or the Industrial Workers of the World.

This may well be an important reason for Republican domination of national politics after the Civil War. The GOP was divided between two wings, but both had political goals that required them to cooperate with similar-minded people in other parts of the country. First there were the Radical Republicans, who were determined to punish the South for slavery and for launching the war. Then there were the expansionists, seeking tariffs and credit legislation that would build up industry. For both this meant concentration on the Congress and the Presidency. The Republicans dominated national politics because they wanted to dominate national policies. The only really vital force among the Democrats —the Irish machines—did not share the same desire—or at least did not share it with the same intensity. Their base was urban, and even had they wished to do so, they had no way of penetrating the voters in rural or small-town areas. These areas were predominant in America until the late 1920s. Under such circumstances, there could be only one winner of the White House.

There were divisions within the Republican Party upon which the Irish skills might have been exercised had the city bosses wanted to do so. One that began to develop early was the growing antagonism of the farmers toward an industrial economy. Independent farmers have a difficult time in an industrial society. Everything they buy comes from manufacturers that can control their production to ensure maximum profits. But everything they grow is dumped upon an uncontrolled market, where farm prices can be depressed even when the price of factory goods is going up. In addition, the railroad trusts had full power to squeeze them in the shipment of their crops to market. The process is described graphically in the novel *The Octopus* by Frank Norris. Bitterness became widespread in the farm belt, whose spokesman was William Jennings Bryan, the orator from Nebraska. Bryan became the perennial Democratic Presidential candidate, able to get the Democratic nominations because most men did not want the job very badly. Furthermore, his major political program—low interest rates through bimetallism—was not divisive in the party. Later came the Progressive and Farmer-Labor Party revolts, mostly abortive, because the urban politicians did not lend a helping hand.

Of course, this situation could not last forever. The country was growing in population, and the various segments of America's economy were becoming more dependent upon each other. Cities were developing into unlivable areas as the pace of immigration mounted. More was needed in terms of caring for people who were down on their luck. From a social standpoint, the United States was becoming unwieldy.

This was not immediately apparent, however. To the machines, the development of the cities looked good: constantly expanding quarters for people to occupy; constantly expanding transportation lines to create jobs; constantly growing needs for police and firefighters; culminating in constantly expanding sources for votes. The social services of the machine could be financed by huge public payrolls and by kickbacks from street paving, bridge building, and house-construction contractors. The goose seemed not only to be laying golden eggs but providing new and bigger geese.

Of course, there were setbacks. Around the turn of the century, major recessions—called panics—cut off many payrolls. But they did not last very long. The bosses thought they had a self-perpetuating machine. What they had not counted upon was the trend within the cities toward becoming more and more dependent on other cities and on the countryside. In short, the unit of their power became too small.

Chapter 9

♣

The THRESHOLD of the NATIONAL STAGE

SEVENTY-NINE YEARS HAVE PASSED SINCE IT HAPPENED BUT A review of the events in the Triangle Shirtwaist Fire can still send cold chills down the spine of anyone of sensibility. The intervening time span has brought us the monstrosities of World Wars I and II, the massacre of the Armenians, the Holocaust that sent millions of Jews to firing squads and the gas chambers, the mass starvations in the Ukraine and Ethiopia. This has truly been the century of man's inhumanity to man. We have become numb over the sheer enormity of figures that convert sadistic butchery to statistics. But the numbness disappears and becomes a stabbing pain when we read about the 150 young women who died screaming in the flames or plunging to concrete sidewalks four to six stories below.

There were enough people involved—at least 600 trapped in the building when the fire began—to convey the horrors of massive death. But at the same time, the numbers were sufficiently small to give all who watched or read a sense of "that might have been me." *The New York Times* of March 26, 1911, used half of its front page and extensive portions of five inside pages for pictures and stories of the disaster. There were detailed accounts of women jumping from windows despite crowds on the street urging them not to make the dive. For days afterward the specific events were explored—the provision of just one fire escape in a location where it was useless, the dead bodies piled up in the elevator shaft, the corpses that littered the street (five were never identified), the locked doors.

New York had seen many tenement fires in the preceding years. The garment industry had become a basic factor in the city's life, and this meant sweat shops, where workers were jammed into airless rooms and surrounded by highly inflammable material.

[99]

Most of these fires, however, had simply been ignored by the authorities and by the nongarment-worker populace. Few actually produced more than one or two casualties. The Triangle Shirtwaist fire was too big to be ignored. Furthermore, even though most of the workers were Jewish and Italian, they were still Tammany constituents, and however much the sachems had exploited their political connections to add to their own personal fortunes, they were still acutely conscious of their power base and the necessity for maintaining it intact.

It took very little reflection for them to realize that they were helpless to deal with such situations within the city limits. The City Council could easily write and pass protective labor laws, but what good were they outside the boundaries? Obviously, the sweat-shop operator who wanted to ignore inconvenient regulations could easily move to nearby New Jersey or to suburbs, where he was still within reach of the New York City labor market. Cheap mass transportation had made it possible to draw on a much wider spread pool of workers than in the days when labor, management, and plant equipment all had to be within the same neighborhood.

Fortunately for the development of the Irish machines, there had also been changes in other aspects of American life as well.

Some of these changes were not the sort that could be analyzed statistically or physically. For example, a new type of aristocrat was rising in the United States. There were men—such as Franklin D. Roosevelt—whose money came from forebears buried so deep in the past that they themselves had lost the instinct for rapacity that produced it in the first place. At about the same time there began to emerge second or third generation Irish politicians who had lost the sense of desperation that had characterized the Potato Famine refugees. Many of them had succeeded in acquiring an education, and even those who had not, such as Al Smith—whose "college" was the Fulton Street fish market—had become impatient with the parochialism of the old machines and wanted to play their roles on a larger stage.

It is doubtful that any single event ever "causes" historical changes. But frequently it acts as a catalyst, revealing to members of society that they are sharing passionate feelings with others. The Triangle Fire was in that category. As a catalyst, it resulted in state legislative investigations and protective labor laws that made New York virtually a model for other states to emulate. But its most important effect was to arrange a marriage between the Irish machines and liberal reformers—the wealthy and the educated—which was to result in a far-reaching revolution twenty-two years later. It put together the basic elements of the New Deal, which, when all the confusing alphabetical agencies it created were stripped away, came down to a conviction that government had not only a right but an obligation to help individual citizens when they were in trouble.

It is instructive to follow the activities of Al Smith at this point. He was a devoted Tammany man—honest but dedicated to the organization. He had been elected to the State Assembly where, with another—but non-Irish—Tammanyite, Robert F. Wagner, he put together a committee to study factory conditions with a staff directed by Frances Perkins, destined to become the first woman in American history to achieve a cabinet post—Secretary of Labor. The investigation had some backing from Tammany leader Charles F. Murphy. And one of the principal helpers in this enterprise was the Hudson Valley aristocrat Franklin D. Roosevelt. Wagner was chairman and Smith vice chairman, and they spent months in hearings and personal investigations. For Smith, it was an experience that broadened his horizons radically. He traveled all over the state and saw, at first hand, its problems. Never again would he be happy totally within the city. He became so well versed in what was going on that, when he participated in a Constitutional Convention in 1915, Elihu Root described him as the best-informed delegate on the business of New York as a whole.

There was a temporary hiatus in the alliance among Roosevelt, Wagner, and Smith. FDR joined the Wilson administration as assistant secretary of the navy; Wagner was placed on the New York Supreme Court bench, and Smith, in his last fling at purely city politics, became sheriff of New York County. But it was not long before the three were back together again, beginning in 1919 when Smith became governor of New York State.

The transition from parochialism to the state scene and then the national was not confined solely to New York. In 1910, an Irish machine headed by "Jim" Smith was credited with placing Woodrow Wilson in the governor's mansion in New Jersey. And two years later, a last-minute switch by Irish bosses Tom Taggart of Indiana and Roger Sullivan of Illinois made possible Wilson's nomination as Democratic candidate for the Presidency. It was a new day for the Irish and a long road from the Potato Famine.

The support of Wilson gained very little for the Irish except the appointment of Joseph Tumulty as his personal secretary. Tumulty, a lawyer and probably the highest ranking Irishman in the Federal government up to the Wilson administration, performed brilliantly. He offset the cold, unyielding personality of his boss, who was the kind of man who could not suffer a fool at all, let alone gladly. Tumulty knew how to deal with Congress, the press, and patronage, and his loyalty echoed the fanatical devotion of the Gaelic clansmen toward their chief. But this was not enough. The President considered firing him on a number of occasions and finally rejected him altogether.

Wilson was basically the embodiment of the stereotype for an Anglican dean. He was highly cerebral and lacked the elementary emotional responses that go with good fellowship. He also, without fully understanding the implications, had a picture of the United States founded on the political, social, and literary traditions of Great Britain. This hampered him in many respects. He never understood why the Democrats in Congress did not rally behind all of his measures, because he confused the Presidency with the office of Prime Minister. His confusion on this point was compounded by the "honeymoon" period of his first two years in office when a very remarkable Senate Democratic Leader—John W. Kern, of Indiana—succeeded in ramming all his programs through the Chamber.

The most important of the Wilson personality failures, how-

[102]

ever, was his lack of understanding of the ethnic groups who made up so much of the American scene. To him, Irish-Americans, Polish-Americans, Italian-Americans, German-Americans, and Swedish-Americans were "hyphenates." The thought never seemed to have crossed his mind that his own admiration for British institutions could easily have earned him the hyphenated tag "Anglo-American." He was basically a WASP reformer, who detested the city machines as much for their lack of style as for their venality. He did not understand that they were filling a need—providing much-needed services for people at the bottom of the social ladder.

World War I brought the divisions between Wilson and the Irish politicians to the fore. But even before the United States had entered—when Wilson was still preaching "too proud to fight" and maintaining a strict neutrality—evidence of his feeling flashed from time to time. Shannon quotes a Wilson speech in which he praised the Revolutionary War hero John Barry as an Irishman whose "heart crossed the Atlantic with him." He described other Americans, with little doubt as to his meaning, as needing "hyphens in their names because only part of them has come over." Once the United States entered the war, hyphenated Americanism became something of a national obsession. Of course, most of the obloquy was directed against German-Americans. It was a period when sauerkraut became "Liberty cabbage" and home-front warriors demonstrated their patriotism by pouring yellow paint over a statue of Goethe in Chicago's Lincoln Park. But a good deal of it was directed against the Irish as well.

The war actually gave the American Irish a tough time. As Eamon de Valera pointed out, they were really American, and their Irishness had become to some extent a question of sentimentality. They were no longer a nation in exile; they were here to stay. But they still held sentimental ties to the past, one of which was virulent hatred of England. To them American participation in the war meant helping Perfidious Albion—when many could remember the bitterness in their grandfathers' voices as they spoke of "the Sassenachs." Nevertheless, when the showdown finally came, Irish-Americans were far more American than Irish. By 1916, a majority were probably third generation who had sunk deep roots in American soil.

The Irish were still somewhat set apart, but their loyalties were toward South Boston and Back of the Yards in Chicago, rather than to County Clare or Mayo. They dressed like Americans, played like Americans, and ate like Americans. The traditional dish in the Irish ghettoes was corned beef and cabbage—virtually unknown in the land of their ancestors. Furthermore, they were beginning to move up the ladder in American society. There was more involved than a mere capture of city political machinery. There were other forms of recognition much more crucial. Prize-fighters John L. Sullivan and Gentleman Jim Corbett were heroes to Americans with impeccable WASP ancestry. The Irish-American writer Finley Peter Dunne had reached an ever-widening audience since the late 1890s, and everywhere was the Irish cop—a figure viewed with considerable affection.

Had the war remained solely a contest between Germany and England, there might have been considerable sentiment for the German side. (After all, it did open the way for a serious uprising in Dublin.) But once the United States entered the conflict, there was no question about where the majority of the Irish stood. Indeed, many of them felt more grateful to the United States than the WASPs. Their ancestors, after all, had found refuges from disaster in Boston and New York and Philadelphia.

What feelings of alienation remained on the part of the Irish translated into a burning desire to prove their Americanism. The Hearst newspaper chain, which bore down heavily on devotion to flag and country, owed much of its success to the ethnic reader who was anxious to erase any appearance of being a "greenhorn"—one of the nastiest words in the American lexicon of the time. Woodrow Wilson's hyphenates were probably more deeply in love with their adopted country than he was. They wanted to show their fierce devotion by fighting for their nation in battle.

Like the Japanese from Hawaii in the Second World War, the

Irish ran up an impressive military record. The Fighting 69th—a New York infantry regiment that had traditionally been Irish— saw the heaviest fighting of any American unit, earning battle streamers in the campaigns of Champagne-Meuse, Aisne-Marne, Saint-Mihiel, Meuse-Argonne, and Lorraine. Wartime casualties took one third of the total that left for France, and in the victory parade in New York after the war, the banners of the 69th bore 615 gold stars.

The World War I years set the stage for the sudden, upward surge of the American Irish in the 1920s. They had been introduced to statewide politics in the period of the Triangle Shirtwaist fire. This had given leaders such as Al Smith an opportunity to see the world—or at least a part of the world—outside New York City. In and of itself, the war did not extend Irish political experience, but it gave Irish lads from the streets of New York, Boston, Chicago, and San Francisco an opportunity to work with young men from other areas. One of the few good effects of war is to promote comradeship among people who normally would know nothing about each other. World War I helped merge the politicians' Irish base with the general population of the United States.

The upward thrust of the Irish became apparent almost as soon as the war was over. In January 1919, Al Smith was inaugurated as governor of New York and launched a program of social reform. It included health and maternity insurance, pure milk for children, better hospitals for the sick and the insane. In effect, he was trying to make social services an official governmental function, rather than favors performed by machine politicians in exchange for votes.

But Al Smith went further than that. His belief in free thought was passionate, visceral, learned from life and not from literature. He became a champion of free speech in the midst of the Great Red Scare that swept America in the early 1920s. In 1914, he fought unsuccessfully against the denial of seats in the New York State Assembly to duly elected Socialists. With somewhat more success, he also resisted efforts to license teachers because of their political beliefs and to institute censorship of books, theaters, and motion pictures. In those days very few voices were raised in defense of unorthodox views, and thus the man from the Fulton Street fish market was heard all the more distinctly.

Of greater significance for the immediate future was Smith's stated opposition to Prohibition and the Ku Klux Klan, both of which were solidly supported by the Democrats of the South. As governor, he succeeded in persuading the legislature to repeal New York's own prohibition act. It is not clear whether he realized that by doing so he was setting the stage for the battle over the soul of the Democratic Party, which was one of the major political dramas of the 1920s.

As long as the Irish were interested only in the cities they were indifferent to the Southern branch of their party. But once it became apparent that the Democratic Party could elect a President and that the Irish machines could play a role in that election, the terms of the combat changed. The Democratic Party could not really be a national party until it came to terms with the North–South split. When the Irish broke out of the cities and joined forces with such liberals as Franklin D. Roosevelt and Frances Perkins, the showdowns of 1924 and 1928 became inevitable.

Another factor that had to be fed into the equation was the Anglo-Irish Treaty of 1921—a document which, in effect, gave Ireland Dominion status. This did not satisfy the Irish, but it did raise basic questions as to the wisdom of continued revolts in the homeland *and* continued support of those revolts by the Irish in the United States. It was one thing to consider oneself a nation in exile, the feeling fostered by continued British rule. But when the reins of English power began to relax, a different situation was created. It became a choice between going back to Ireland or accepting (psychologically) the full obligations of American citizenship. Had such options been offered in the 1850s and the 1860s, there is little doubt as to the answer. But in the 1920s, going back was a ludicrous idea.

Basically, the national pattern of Irish-American development followed the pattern of New York. The second, third, and fourth generation of Irish-Americans lived lives irrevocably tied to the

United States. They had gone to school in its cities; some of them had attended major universities; some of them were making big money (principally in contracting and law); some of them (F. Scott Fitzgerald, for example) were becoming major literary figures— not by writing about the sorrows of Ireland and the cruelties of Strongbow but about the current American scene.

In the political field, Irish names began to bob up in political roles, but not in "city boss" contexts. Senators Tom Walsh of Montana and David I. Walsh of Massachusetts were examples. These were men with vision. Both of them, as well as Smith and other idealistic Irish politicians, still relied upon the bossed machines to turn out the city vote, but they had things they wanted to do for people *after* they were elected.

The acceptance of the Irish by the dominant WASP leaders was still far from complete. Money, political power, and literary recognition were not enough to insure acceptance to the more exclusive clubs in New York or Boston. Brahmins and Anglican deans might attend a performance of Eugene O'Neill's *The Hairy Ape*, but his name still did not appear on guest lists for the Lowells, the Cabots, or the Astors. Still, the walls were crumbling rapidly. The 1920s became the era in which they began to go altogether. It was not apparent at the time, but the fact remained that Irish success was paving the way for putting the Irish politician out of business.

Chapter 10
♣
PURGATION

PRESIDENTIAL POLITICS, LIKE THE SUN IN THE DAYTIME SKY, TENDS to blot out the surrounding universe. The health of a political party is usually gauged by its occupation of the White House in Washington, D.C. By that standard, the 1920s were years of disaster for both the Democratic Party and the Northern machine politicians attempting to step onto the national stage. There was never a chance for a Democratic electoral triumph, and to make matters more humiliating, the Republican majorities were far greater than had been anticipated. The virtually preordained elections of Harding, Coolidge, and Hoover struck many observers as extra shovelsful of dirt dumped on the grave of a moribund political party. Burial had begun before breathing had stopped.

The low esteem in which the Democratic Party was held was shortsighted indeed. A careful look at political races below the level of the Presidency would have revealed that the Democrats were building a solid base in the states. The real gravedigging was going on among the Republicans. The GOP was in the preliminary stages of the split that was to render it so impotent for the two decades that followed Franklin Delano Roosevelt's 1932 triumph. But this split was not so apparent in the 1920s, and whenever it did surface, it was discounted because of the Republican Presidential successes.

The reality was that neither party was being "buried." The nation was going through one of its great periods of social and economic transitions, and both parties were torn by shifting constituencies. By the 1920s, the United States had crossed the magic line that categorized a majority of the population as rural. The American way of life was rapidly becoming urban, with agriculture relegated to the role of serving the people in the cities. A man

[111]

named Henry Ford had succeeded in wedding technology to a high-speed production, and the assembly line had come to America. In addition, further technological advances had made it possible to construct small and cheap radio sets. It was a brand new world.

The technological advances gave Americans far more than new toys to play with. The automobile meant mobility, and the radio unified people hundreds of miles apart. Technology also came to the farm, bringing machinery that increased productivity. Of course, it was expensive. Those farmers who could afford it increased their income—at least at first—but there were many who could not afford it. Furthermore, there was another drawback. The people who produced farm machinery could control their market, so that their production would yield the highest possible return. But the people who used the machinery to raise crops could not control their market. Ultimately, this resulted in an intolerable squeeze on the farmer.

In 1924 the problem of the farmers produced the Progressive Party, most of whose members were from the Republican prairie states, represented by men like Bob LaFollette. There was a sprinkling of Democrats, such as Burton K. Wheeler of Montana, La Follette's running mate in the 1924 Presidential election. The Progressives were regarded, properly so, as a split from the Republicans, but the split did very little damage. Despite some economic setbacks in the very early twenties, the Northern urban areas felt fairly secure, because of the rise in employment sparked by automobiles. In the election, the Republican ticket attracted 2.5 million more votes than the Democratic and Progressive tickets combined.

The problems of the Democrats were far more excruciating. They arose out of the emotional wave of war weariness that swept the nation after World War I, exacerbated by the changing facts of daily life, which were having their harshest impact on Protestant America. This was translated into an antiforeign crusade that took many forms: rejection of the League of Nations, Prohibition, approval of the Ku Klux Klan, disapproval of immigrants, and the Jazz Age. In short, America's traditionalists were afraid their way of life was slipping into limbo.

World War I had introduced many Americans to European cultures that had been alien to their way of life. For the intellectuals of the 1920s, this was a heady experience, which resulted in pilgrimages to Paris. But the new ideas that were brought back both by the returning troops and the intellectuals were not welcomed by WASP America. They deplored the world that was springing up around them and blamed it on the immigrants from Ireland and Southern and Eastern Europe, who—in this WASPish view— had brought evil into paradise.

There is no evidence whatsoever that the United States had been abstemious as a nation prior to the influx of the "foreigners." In fact, the evidence points quite the other way. But beginning in the early part of the twentieth century, a belief became almost universally accepted among Protestants that indulgence in liquor was a vice of people with non-WASP names. After the passage of the Eighteenth Amendment and the Volstead (enforcing) Act, this was translated into a conviction that bootleggers and other violators were not really "Americans." There were strong religious overtones to this idea and in 1921, the evangelist Billy Sunday said that any list of bootleggers and other offshoots of the booze racket "reads like a page of directories from Italy and Greece." There was a certain logic to his claim, since the bootleg gangs who supplied the illegal liquor were largely ethnic. He omitted to mention the fact, however, that their customers were, by and large, WASP.

The Prohibition forces were almost completely under the control of fundamentalist or conservative Protestant denominations. In the South, the stronghold of the Baptist church, support of Prohibition was virtually the same as going to church on Sunday and presenting youngsters for Baptism at the proper age. This did not prevent any Southerner who wanted a drink from getting a drink. But it was an effective bar to any political candidate who stated publicly that Prohibition should be repealed. There was a widespread quip at the time: Southerners would vote for Prohibition as long as they could stagger to the polls.

It was taken for granted by the fundamentalists that booze and the Catholic Church were synonymous. This is what tied the Prohibition issue to the Ku Klux Klan, which had one of its periodic resurgences in Atlanta in 1919. In 1922 it was taken over by a Dallas dentist named Hiram Evans, who styled himself as the Imperial Wizard. In earlier incarnations, the Klan had devoted its efforts to keeping blacks in submission, but the new Klan, under Evans, directed its energies against Catholics and Jews. It was remarkably successful in a number of states, especially Indiana, where it fell just short of political control.

The power of the Klan in the twenties became enormous. Evans based the organization on bigotry, but he buttressed it with economic perquisites that reinforced the loyalty of members. In small towns in Indiana, for example, it became standard for enterprises owned by Klan members to have the word "American" in their titles: the American Restaurant or the American Garage or the American Laundry. This meant full patronage from local klansmen and boycotts of any merchant who did not belong. Such economic power could easily be converted to political power, and outside of a few big cities of the North, politicians—even politicians who did not agree with Klan principles—walked warily. In the Catholic centers of population, of course, opposition to the Klan was a must. After all, politicians connected with the society did not even pretend to tolerance. Senator Tom Heflin of Alabama stated the Klan belief succinctly when he said: "God has set up this great patriotic organization to unmask Popery."

The Democratic Party felt the full force of the battle between the fundamentalists and the machines as early as the 1920 convention. William Jennings Bryan, the perennial Democratic Presidential candidate, showed up with a platform plank committing the Democrats to strict enforcement of Prohibition. He was opposed by a Tammany spokesman, Bourke Cokran, who introduced a resolution to permit the sale and consumption of light wines and beer. Both resolutions were defeated in convention votes, and the final platform said nothing whatsoever about Prohibition. But that did not put an end to the argument. The ultimate nomination of James Cox of Ohio for the Presidency was regarded as a "wet" victory, for which the party had to pay dearly. For one thing, it cost the electioneering talents of Bryan.

The 1920 election resulted in a staggering defeat for the Democrats. Harding received 16 million votes, Cox 9 million, and the Socialist Debs 941,827. This was something of a paradox, since Harding could hardly be regarded as a role model for fundamentalism. His love of liquor, poker, and women was notorious, and gossip about his extracurricular doings was the mainstay of conversation in Washington during his administration. But it did not matter. The disarray of the Democrats was so great that they might have lost even had a Tammany committee been appointed to count the ballots. The party had severe internal problems, and it occurred to very few either inside or outside the political arena that it might be undergoing conditioning for the 1930s.

The highwater mark of the nativist drive was reached with the passage of immigration restriction acts of 1921 and 1924, the latter being the more severe. These acts established the quota system, whose purpose was to cut down drastically the flow of immigrants from Eastern and Southern Europe, without affecting the number that could enter from the British Isles. (The framers of the acts were not concerned about Irish or Northern European immigration, which had not been high for two decades.) There were long-term implications to these measures. Not only did they militate against the supplanting of the WASPs. They also reduced the ranks of the armies who supported the machine bosses. A steady supply of immigrants was essential to them, and after 1924, the supply began to dwindle.

The 1920 debacle at the polls did not persuade either the Northern machines or the Southern Baptists to call off their warfare. They were still loyal to the Democratic Party, because they dared not risk their political structures by imposing name changes. But they were not at all prepared to compromise in any direction—a no-win situation. As the party members approached the 1924 convention in New York City, all the omens pointed to a savage political battle. The convention itself bore out the omens. The convention remains today a classic example of a political party nominating its candidate under conditions that made it absolutely impossible for him to win.

The conservative wing of the Democratic Party preceded the convention by sounding out a long list of possible candidates, including, surprisingly enough, Henry Ford, whose antagonism to Jews and Catholics had strong appeal to the Southern fundamentalists. It did not take very long, however, for their support to shift to William Gibbs McAdoo, Wilson's Secretary of the Treasury. McAdoo, a California lawyer who had practiced in New York, had been born in Georgia and educated in Tennessee, so pro-Klan delegates were certain of where he stood on the basic issues: pro-Klan, anti-Tammany. The assumption that he was pro-Klan was probably untrue, but he did nothing to dispel it. (He was trying to duck the issue altogether as did the man who ultimately received the nomination—John W. Davis of West Virginia.)

The anti-Klan forces came down to a choice between Al Smith and James Cox. There was absolutely no doubt now as to where either side stood: McAdoo for the Klan, and Smith-Cox for Tammany—choices that would have inevitably led to an open split in the Democratic Party. The battle lines that were drawn between McAdoo forces on the one side and Smith-Cox on the other seemed to have no conceivable conclusion other than the total victory for one side and a total, and unacceptable, defeat for the other. Convention managers sought to head off *Götterdämmerung* with a platform plank that condemned bigotry and efforts to sow the seeds of racial discord but did not specify the Ku Klux Klan. It was a well-written document that might have received grudging acceptance in an earlier period. But the dynamics of the controversy had outstripped all efforts at compromise.

The showdown came in a floor fight over an amendment condemning "secret political societies of all kinds" and pledging the Democratic Party "to oppose any effort on the part of the Ku

Klux Klan or any organization to interfere with the religious liberty or political freedom of any citizen. . . ." Instead of compromise the mere reading of the amendment touched off an uproar and opened up a debate that may well have been the most violent battle inside a convention hall in American history. There were not only yells and screams and catcalls but fistfights on the floor itself.

McAdoo himself hid out in a hotel room, where he could not be reached for comment, and his campaign manager got out of the way as fast as he could. It made no difference. The McAdoo delegates were against the anti-Klan plank, and either assumed— or didn't care—that their candidate agreed with them. The Smith-Cox forces were in better shape, because their leaders were not trying to straddle the issue. The voices of compromise were drowned out but still existed in terms of votes. The final roll call defeated the amendment by one vote—541 and 3/20 to 542 and 3/20. (In the 1920s, fractionalization of convention votes was carried to ridiculous extremes.) More important than the plank, however, was the obvious fact that the biggest losers were McAdoo, Smith, and Cox. The heated debate had served the purpose of exhausting emotions; no one wanted to renew the knock-down-and-drag-out conflict. The three top candidates were put into nomination and led the voting for 100 ballots. But Cox finally withdrew his nomination and McAdoo released his delegates, leaving Smith to search for a compromise. Early harmony efforts collapsed, but eventually Cox, who had absented himself from the convention despite the strength of his candidacy, traveled to New York and threw his weight behind Davis. The West Virginian, who had not been spattered by the political gore of the Ku Klux Klan fight, was nominated on the 103rd ballot.

There was no doubt about the final result. The Northern political machines had waged a pitched battle against the Southerners, and the outcome had been even. Neither side could be overwhelmed, but neither side had the strength to deliver a knockout punch. However, the Northern machines had gained allies and were obviously on the upward track in terms of national politics, whereas the Southern Democrats had picked up no significant new strength and had suffered some losses in the battle. The decision was a tie, but obviously there was going to be a rematch someday—analogous to an aging, champion prizefighter eking out a draw with a younger opponent, whom he would have to face again all too soon.

One of the most important events at the convention was the nomination of Smith by Franklin D. Roosevelt, borrowing Wordsworth's haunting phrase to describe the Tammany man as "the Happy Warrior of the political battlefield." The alliance between Tammany (or, at least, the reform wing of Tammany) and the liberal patricians was still solid, each giving the other constituencies that would grow even larger in the years to come. To that must be added a series of speeches opposing the Klan, made by a remarkable trio. One was Bainbridge Colby of New York, like Roosevelt an aristocrat and a pillar of Eastern society. The second was David I. Walsh, a Massachusetts Irishman who sounded like a Mick but who had transcended ward politics to become a Senator of the United States. The third was Edmund H. Moore, a national committeeman from Ohio, a pious Protestant and definitely not the creation of ward politics. These were only three men, but they stood as symbols of what was to come in politics. They opposed the Klan bluntly as incompatible with America's freedoms and well-being.

The McAdoo forces had nothing similar to their credit. Instead, the fighting revealed vulnerable gaps in their political armor. One of the most obvious was Senator Oscar Underwood, favorite-son candidate from Alabama, who announced upon his arrival in New York that his delegation would sponsor an anti-Klan resolution or support any that was offered. He was a man marked for political oblivion, but the mere fact that men of his temperament could be elected to a statewide office from one of the keystones of the Confederacy was significant. He was also opposed to Prohibition. At the time, Underwood hardly represented the thinking of the South, but it was clear that the solid, segregationist structure built by Dixie was beginning to crack. Further evidence was provided by an unexpected anti-Klan speech from Andrew D. Erwin,

UNITED STATES - WORKING FOR IT.

AMERICAN GOLD.

IRELAND - WAITING FOR IT

This caricature appeared in the American humor magazine Puck *in the late nineteenth century. Although savagely anti-Irish, it depicted a reality of Irish life. The "letter from America" haunted the thoughts of many Irish in the Western Counties.* (Courtesy of The John F. Kennedy Library)

In the 1850s and '60s respectable WASP society regarded the Irish as bestial brawlers with faces like baboons and tastes for nothing but blood and rum. This cartoon by Thomas Nast represents the Celtic face in the eyes of non-Irish America. (Courtesy of The John F. Kennedy Library)

ST. PATRICKS DAY 1867.

RUM — BRUTAL ATTACK ON THE POLICE. "THE DAY WE CELEBRATE." IRISH RIOT. Th. Nast. BLOOD.

BOSS TWEED.

"Boss" Tweed was Scots rather than Irish, but he virtually invented the Irish political machine, including the springboard that catapulted the Irish to power—control of the police and fire departments. Here he appears as the foreman of a fire department team in his early days. (Courtesy of The Bettmann Archive)

The crash of the Tweed Ring reverberated throughout American political circles. The boodlery practiced by him and his henchmen—mostly Irish—was so enormous that even the honest members of the Irish machines were tainted with a reputation of corruption. (Courtesy of The Bettmann Archive)

Despite the fall of Boss Tweed and his henchmen, Tammany Hall survived by elevating to the post of Grand Sachem "Honest John" Kelly, who really was honest. (Courtesy of The Bettmann Archive)

Tammany's Grand Sachem.

JOHN KELLY.

SHERIFF'S OFFICE

OF THE CITY AND COUNTY OF NEW YORK.

December 6th, 1875.

$10,000 Reward.

The above reward will be paid for the apprehension and delivery to the undersigned, or his proper agents, of

WM. M. TWEED,

Who escaped from the Jailor of the City and County of New York, on Saturday, December 4th, 1875. At the time of his escape he was under indictment for Forgery and other crimes, and was under arrest in civil actions in which bail had been fixed by the Court at the amount of Four Million Dollars.

The following is a Description of said WM. M. TWEED:

He is about fifty-five years of age, about five feet eleven inches high, will weigh about two hundred and eighty pounds, very portly, ruddy complexion, has rather large, coarse, prominent features and large prominent nose; rather small blue or grey eyes, grey hair, from originally auburn color; head nearly bald on top from forehead back to crown, and bare part of ruddy color; head projecting toward the crown. His beard may be removed or dyed, and he may wear a wig or be otherwise disguised. His photograph is attached.

WILLIAM C. CONNER,
Sheriff.

George Washington Plunkitt, one of the most outspoken Irish bosses, made no effort to hide his acquisitive instincts. When he retired, he was asked how he had accumulated so much money on small city salaries. His classic response was "I seen my opportunities and took advantage of them." He is shown here in about 1905, perched on his favorite shoeshine stand. (Copyright The Chicago Tribune Company, all rights reserved. Used with permission.)

AWAITING THE MORROW

This cartoon from the Boston Post *caricatures "Honey John" Fitzgerald's successful comeback in 1910, backed by Martin Lomasney and a string of ward heelers. Honey Fitz, at the telescope, emerged as the major figure of the city's politics.* (Courtesy of The John F. Kennedy Library)

Martin Lomasney was a major powerhouse in Boston in the early part of this century. Here he is pictured in some spellbinding oratory.
(Courtesy of the Boston Public Library, Print Department)

Honey Fitz was a man ahead of his times in many respects. Here he is seen with Graham White, a loyal retainer, in an early airplane.
(Courtesy of the Boston Public Library, Print Department)

The sense of family was deeply rooted in Irish politicians. Here James Michael Curley attends the dedication of an altar to his first wife. (Courtesy of the Boston Public Library, Print Department)

In the history of Irish machine bosses, there was no more appealing character than Al Smith. He worked his way up from the slums of New York City. Honest, intelligent, and forceful, he displayed a remarkable grasp of economic and social problems, which made him a successful governor. Nominated for the Presidency in 1928, he was smothered by one of the worst campaigns of bigotry in American history. Here he campaigns for Franklin D. Roosevelt in 1932. (Copyright The Chicago Tribune Company, all rights reserved. Used with permission.)

It would be difficult to find two bosses more dissimilar than Frank Hague of Jersey City (second from left) and Ed Kelly of Chicago (far right). Heavyhanded and dictatorial, Hague proclaimed that in Jersey City: "I am the law." Kelly controlled Chicago politics quietly and deftly. The two men did get together, however, at the opening Chicago Cubs game in 1935. Immediately to Hague's right sits Jake Arvey, representing the rising Jewish power in the city, and between Hague and Kelly is Judge John J. Sullivan. (Copyright The Chicago Tribune Company, all rights reserved. Used with permission.)

The Irish machines selected candidates for the Senate or the Presidency with care. This picture, taken at the 1936 Democratic National Convention, shows Harry S Truman, one of the most honorable and honest men who ever entered the White House, with his sponsor, Thomas J. Pendergast, who was later convicted for misuse of office. LEFT TO RIGHT: *Truman, Pendergast, James P. Aylward, James A. Farley, N. G. Robinson, and David A. Fitzgerald.* (Courtesy of Harry S Truman Library)

When it came to Irish politicians, Franklin Delano Roosevelt discriminated only between those who could and could not deliver the vote. In the Massachusetts Presidential primary of 1932, James Michael Curley backed FDR and Senator David I. Walsh backed Al Smith. Walsh and Smith won. When Roosevelt was elected President, he sent Curley some nice letters and turned Federal patronage over to Walsh, pictured here on his way to a political meeting. (Courtesy of the Boston Public Library, Print Department)

Franklin Delano Roosevelt used the Irish machine bosses to elevate him to the Presidency and keep him in the White House, but very few of them were actually his friends. One of the exceptions was the soft-spoken but potent mayor of Chicago, Ed Kelly, shown here with the President and Mrs. Roosevelt on the ride to the Chicago Stadium, where FDR accepted the Democratic renomination. (Copyright The Chicago Tribune Company, all rights reserved. Used with permission.)

Under Richard J. Daley, Irish power in Chicago approached regal proportions, and politicians, regardless of their rank, treated him as a king. Here he leads the 1968 St. Patrick's Day parade in Chicago, flanked by Thomas Tierney, mayor of Galway, Ireland, and Pat O'Brien, the beloved movie star. (Copyright The Chicago Tribune Company, all rights reserved. Used with permission.)

By the time John F. Kennedy entered the political arena, Lomasney was gone but Honey Fitz and Curley were still potent. Here the future President is seen with Honey Fitz to his left and Curley to his right—good guides for the road to the White House. (Courtesy of the Boston Public Library, Print Department)

Rallying the troops for the final push, John F. Kennedy addresses his followers in the Boston Garden just before his election in 1960. The final margin of victory was thin—and was probably delivered by Richard J. Daley of Chicago. (Courtesy of the Boston Public Library, Print Department)

It was a long road from the ward to the White House, ending in 1961, 113 years after the potato blight drove famine victims to the United States. Here John F. Kennedy takes the Presidential oath of office. (Courtesy of The John F. Kennedy Library)

editor of the Athens, Georgia, *Banner-Herald*, whose father had been an officer in the Confederate Army and who was a Presbyterian of Scotch-Irish descent (not the stuff out of which Irish political machines were made). Other Georgia delegates made it clear that they shared his sentiments.

What was especially noteworthy was the lack of clear-cut *pro-Klan* speeches at the convention. Those who spoke against the resolution did so either on the grounds that they were seeking to avoid a split in the convention or that it was somehow "unfair" to single out one group for condemnation. The principal oration along these lines was delivered by William Jennings Bryan, who had to pause at least three times while the convention chairman sought to restore order among booing and hissing delegates. The main thrust of the Bryan speech was a depiction of the Klan as a "minor" issue and a plea to reserve the passion engendered by the debate and use it against Republicans.

The Bryan speech was a voice out of the past. The fierce dispute that erupted at the Democratic convention was, in retrospect, essential to the future of the party. Of course, it rendered hopeless any thoughts of achieving the White House in 1924. But it also indicated that the Democratic Party was in the mainstream of history, with the alliances centered around the Irish political machines riding the crest. Had the machine men sidestepped the showdown with the South, the result could well have been the reduction of the Democrats to a small sect that eventually would have lost its grip on the big cities. The 1924 convention was something of a colossal chess gambit—the surrender of an election for an advantageous position that ultimately would sweep the boards. The stage was also set for the high-water mark of the Irish machines in 1928.

Chapter 11

♣

The ROARING TWENTIES

FOR THE CRUDE, HUNGRY, DISEASED REFUGEES FROM THE POTATO Famine who swarmed into the United States in the 1850s, the Decade of the Irish was the 1920s. Those were the years in which the machines consolidated their power not only in the cities, which they ruled already, but in the Democratic Party on a nationwide basis. They were no longer satisfied with perfunctory meetings every four years, which would produce a Presidential candidate whose main virtue was that he would let them alone if, by some fluke, he was elected. They had learned, as a result of the Triangle Shirtwaist fire and other urban disasters, that their ethnic constituents had problems that could not be solved at the city level. They had also produced leaders who were unmistakably Irish—Al Smith and David I. Walsh—but were not content to live within the boundaries of the wards and the City Council chambers. Such men were not poets in the sense of Yeats and Synge, but neither were they boodling pols in the sense of Boss Tweed and George Washington Plunkitt.

The Donnybrook convention of 1924 was a direct result of the new feeling. Basically, it was a challenge to the Bourbons of the South on such issues as Prohibition and the Ku Klux Klan. But behind the ostensible issues was a deeper question that had to be answered. It was whether the Democratic Party would become a truly national political force or would remain a convenient haven for segregationists and small-time grafters. In this struggle, the ostensible issues played the same role that a football plays in a football game. The ball does not *cause* the game, but the game cannot be played without the ball.

The position of the Irish was dictated almost automatically by the position of their power base. The big cities felt the impact

[123]

of social and economic change early and to an accentuated degree. Furthermore, the power base of the city machines had been enhanced by the continuing drift to metropolitan areas, which by 1920 had come to shelter more than 50 percent of the population. The cities did not play the same role south of the Mason-Dixon line in the thinking of politicians. Southern leaders based their strength on what Jim Hogg, a Texas populist governor, once characterized as the people who lived "at the forks of the creek." They were nativist, fundamentalist, and so obsessed by "the Black menace" that they were willing to forgo legislation that would lift them out of an economic morass, as long as they were protected from what they termed "the horrors of miscegenation." Their votes produced officials who were adept at preventing the encroachment of urban ideas into what they called "God's country." The 1920 Democratic convention was a partial setback for the South in the nomination of a man (Cox) who was anti-Klan and anti-Prohibition. But that was only a preliminary skirmish. The big battle of 1924 ended with both sides licking their wounds—in a sense, a draw. But it was a draw between two combatants, and one of them—a holdover from the Old Confederacy—was being overwhelmed by history. It had no way to go but down. The other— the Irish machine politician—was on an upswing to its destined peak. Forces had been set in motion that were irreversible.

The political life of the 1920s cannot be comprehended without placing it against the convulsions that were wracking American society. It was a time of bewildering change—probably the greatest since the birth of the United States factory culture in the mid-nineteenth century. This time there were two revolutions—one in morals and the other in the economics of production and distribution. Institutions that were believed to have the stability of Gibraltar were in disarray. The divisions that were produced went deeper than any before and reached into individual families. As a small child of that period, my most persistent memories are those of the heated arguments between Reedys and younger Mulurneys.

The revolution in morals is now the simpler to comprehend

but at the time, it was the more painful to confront. It had been caused primarily by our dispatch of young Americans to serve in the army overseas. For many it was their first contact with the outer world and they saw many things they liked. They returned to the United States with some strange ideas about sexual mores and with a disinclination to go back to chopping weeds or baling cotton. A song popular at the time was entitled "How Ya Gonna Keep 'Em Down on the Farm, After They've Seen Paree?" It was a prophetic ditty.

The issue most discussed was divorce. My impression (and I must stress that this was the impression of a small child) was that a divorced woman, prior to the war, had about the same social status as a street hooker. If she was a person of some sensibility, she would enter a convent or at least seclude herself from society—any other course of action would strip her of respectability. The position of a divorced man was not quite so extreme, but he was never invited to a home social gathering, where he might strike up an acquaintance with one's sister or daughter. The youngest of my aunts on the Protestant side did get a divorce, and the clucking among her older sisters and aunts made any gathering of the family sound like a barnyard. Ultimately, it was decided that she was not really evil—just scatterbrained—and by the mid-decade, it was forgotten except as a part of family history. Divorce had become so commonplace that it no longer excited comment.

The manner in which women dressed led to even greater fights. It seems that before the war, females were expected to hide their legs *and even their toes* completely after the age of puberty. The older women in my family stuck to the custom, and I somehow got the idea that they had lost their feet and were gliding around on rollers. The younger women would have none of it. Their dresses went to midthigh, their hair was bobbed, they smoked cigarettes, and they drank cocktails. There was the Charleston— a dance that would seem rather innocent in an age accustomed to the lambada. But in the early twenties it was looked upon as the equivalent of a black mass.

The other revolution was somewhat less spectacular but more

enduring in its long-range impact. It began in 1913 with the inauguration of the assembly-line system of manufacture by Henry Ford. Originally, automobiles had been assembled as a single unit. It was an expensive process, as it required a high degree of skill on the part of the workers and a considerable waste of labor time because men had to stand around waiting for their turn to attach parts to the car. The idea of moving the frame down a line flanked by low-skilled workers, who only had to learn how to fasten a single piece in place as the developing car went by, was more than just an efficient way of handling production. It also meant that automobiles could be manufactured so cheaply that they could be made available to a mass market. In turn, that meant that millions of Americans who had previously spent most of their lives within a few miles of their birthplace suddenly found themselves with a degree of mobility on the order of the magic carpet. Until the 1920s, the only peripatetic class in American society had been the hoboes—men who simply could not settle down in one place. Almost overnight, our country became a nation of people in the East moving West and people in the West moving East.

Other developments were just as unsettling—radios, for instance. At first, they were just toys made by young boys out of cigar boxes, a cat's whisker, a galena quartz crystal, and a battery. I put one together myself and spent many evenings trying to pick up a ship on Lake Michigan, which was about all the broadcasting available in the beginning. Gradually professional radio stations appeared on the scene, and manufacturers put radio sets of greater reliability on the market. Overnight, entertainment adapted to radio appeared: dialect comedians in the late 1920s such as Amos and Andy; singers like Rudy Vallee, big bands such as Wayne King. Jewish culture blossomed during the decade, including singers and songwriters who had the whole nation humming. Irving Berlin, Fanny Brice, and Eddie Cantor were better known than the U.S. Presidents of the era.

In times of transition, when there is no clear-cut national will, the spotlight tends to shift to sizable minorities who know what they want. Americans who did care about politics—and there were not too many—could be divided into the traditionalist of the countryside, the small town, and the suburbs, symbolized by Calvin Coolidge, and the Irish machines symbolized by Al Smith. The campaign oratory revolved around a series of "public type" issues such as Prohibition and the Ku Klux Klan. But what put some steam behind the discussions was the desperation of people who felt that the past was slipping away or that the future was too long in arriving. The determining factor was the increase in urbanization, which meant a new style of life.

The city machines began consolidating their power at a rapid pace. My own direct contact with machine politics as something other than an observer was in Chicago, where the Irish did not take over completely until the 1930s. Nevertheless, they had power, which they exercised on a day-to-day basis in running the routine life of the people. There were two reasons they did not assume the total control that Tammany reached in New York. One was the presence of other ethnic groups, which did not have quite their numbers and had come upon the scene at a later point but which had equivalent skill in manipulating votes. They were the Czechs, who lived in a relatively small enclave on the West Side, and the Jews who found a unifying force in the activities of the garment workers' unions. Neither of them engaged in power showdowns with the Irish, but it was clear at an early point that the machine had to reckon with them, and it did.

The other reason why complete control could not be achieved was Big Bill the Builder Thompson, one of the most colorful city mayors the nation ever produced. He lived on a western ranch (even though he was born in Massachusetts), and he affected a cowboy hat whenever he appeared in public. What was really the key to his success, however, was his firm grasp of ethnic politics. In this league he even outdid the Irish and quite possibly taught "the bhoys" a few lessons. His technique was a two-pronged attack against his opponents that invariably won elections: his assaults on England and his reassurances to the ethnic groups that they were real Americans.

To the modern generation, the ethnic hatred of Great Britain that existed in the 1920s is virtually unbelievable. It was the underlying bedrock of unity in Chicago. The hatred ran so deep that it obliterated the lines that normally would have kept all of these groups at each other's throats. When Big Bill charged that King George had written the textbooks used by Chicago schoolchildren, respectable people scoffed at the nonsense. But Wilson's "hyphenated Americans" believed it.

The second prong of his attack was a simple, two-word slogan: "America First." Except for evicting King George from the public school system, he never defined the term or outlined a course of action that would be based upon it. But that didn't matter. The one thing that all the ethnics wanted was to be regarded as 1,000 percent Americans. They were tired of the street warfare that had turned them into Micks, Polacks, Wops, Krauts, and Spades. They hated the upper crust who were outside this arena, but at the same time they wanted to belong to it in terms of riches and status. They thought of themselves as Americans first, and Big Bill summed up their yearnings. In a lifetime spent around the political scene, I have come across no slogan as potent as "America First" was in the 1920s.

By most of the normal rules of politics, Big Bill should have flickered out more quickly than a moist match in a gale. He was a Republican, and most of the people who thought of themselves as Republican despised him as riffraff. *The Chicago Tribune*, the most Republican paper in the United States, refused to support him after he got the Republican nomination even though Colonel McCormick, the publisher, shared his Anglophobia. But in the twenties, he breezed in every time. His opponents ran against him solely for the sake of the publicity, and they didn't get much of that.

The Irish leaders early came to terms with the fact that no one could hate England more fiercely than Big Bill Thompson, and they would only alienate their constituencies by being too vigorous in their opposition. They were practical men, descended from long lines of people who had learned to live with whatever they could get and who knew better than to lose everything by reaching beyond the length of their arm. Furthermore, Thompson was not particularly interested in interfering with them, other than by the occupation of City Hall. He did not disturb the personal fiefs of Bathhouse John Coughlin or Hinky Dink Kenna in the 1st Ward, nor did he make any effort to disarrange the power centers in the police forces and the district attorney's office. His management of the mayoralty office was routine, and his administrations were far less colorful than his campaigns. His Anglophobia was insufficient for him to weather the political storms of the Great Depression, and in a very few years he was completely forgotten. But the machines were still there. Even though they had been unable to defeat him, their organization was more enduring than his oratory.

There were still plenty of divisions among "the bhoys," but these could all be handled with deals. I remember many of my father's conversations on how to match Paddy Bauler and Bathhouse John or Danny (known as Tubbo by the press) Gilbert and Pat Nash. But all it really meant was that leadership at this stage was still collective. It was not until the regime of Ed Kelly that local power became concentrated in Chicago.

A survey of big cities in the nation would have produced, outside of New York, the same results. Of course there was no other Big Bill Thompson to cause trouble. But even if he had had clones, it is probable that the results would have been the same. What the Irish machines had was *organization*, which did not depend upon the presence of a charismatic leader to endure. Therefore, they could indulge in all kinds of intramural rivalry, knowing that loss of a battle did not mean loss of the war. The bottom line was that they were growing stronger in the Democratic Party with each passing day.

In Jersey City, Frank Hague was "the law," and "Uncle Dan" O'Connell had taken over the organization established in Albany, New York, by Patrick McCabe in the late 1890s. In Pittsburgh, David Lawrence was starting his rise to power in the machine that had been established earlier by William McNair. In San Francisco, the Progressive Movement, headed by Hiram Johnson, had taken overall control away from the organization established through

Chris Buckley and carried on by "Pinhead" McCarthy during the period that preceded World War I. But the Irish vote remained potent through control of the police. In one sense, they were even stronger in terms of national Democratic Party control because the reform Democrats went along with Hiram Johnson.

In addition to organizational strength, the machines were picking up more allies as time went on. The alliance between them and the liberal (and wealthy) aristocrats—such as Averell Harriman and Herbert Lehman—had become solidified as the Republican Party had taken on more of the coloration of "big business." At the same time, another potential ally was beginning to shape up—the new breed of American intellectual. The literary motif of the early 1920s was the sense of disillusion through which American artists were looking at the world. What they saw was an emotional wasteland peopled by men and women who were passionate only in greed and had no way to fill in their time other than frenetic activity. The new breed of writers were not muckrakers in the style of Upton Sinclair or Frank Norris in the late 1890s and the early 1900s. They were not savage in their excoriation of man's inhumanity to man. But they were desperate in their search for something in which to believe.

F. Scott Fitzgerald portrayed the hip-flask, raccoon-skin coat, fraternity-drunk parties of the children of the elite. Sinclair Lewis painted in dull grays life in medium-size towns and set forth in such books as *Main Street* and *Babbitt* lives of spiritual misery, from which there was no escape. Eugene O'Neill in two of the most powerful plays of the American stage—*The Hairy Ape* and *The Great God Brown*—told us that we may not be oppressing people any more, but we are casting them into outer darkness where they could be ignored. Ernest Hemingway was praising macho males—either as bullfighters or ambulance drivers during World War I—in a society which he regarded as wimpish and dreary. Walter Lippmann regarded the breakdown of prewar social standards as a crisis and said that he doubted "whether the student can do a greater work for his nation in this grave moment of its history than to detach himself from its preoccupations . . ." The philosophy of pragmatism, expounded most effectively by John Dewey in his book *Human Nature and Conduct*, became the underpinning of the theoretical life of the era. In essence, it held that truth was to be found in context rather than in engraved commandments. Many Americans agreed with the concept but could not find the context.

The intellectuals had little impact upon the politics of the twenties, because reasonably comfortable Americans were absorbed in the stock market prosperity. They voted for Republican Presidents simply because the prosperity was associated with the Republican Party nationally, and the investors did not want to risk losing what they had.

In short, it was a period in which the intellectuals were developing a growing antipathy to what Republicans regarded as their own institution. This did not mean that the literati had very much in common with the Irish politicians. But it did mean that they were quite willing to be part of a coalition *against* the Republicans when the time became ripe. It was not a coalition that could be formed until some crisis precipitated conditions under which it could be won. But all the elements were in place. They only needed a banner around which to rally.

No such event took place until the end of the twenties. So the election and reelection of Republican Presidents became virtually monotonous. Meanwhile, however, the strength of the machines continued to grow and with it a desire to step on a broader stage. Eventually they stepped on that stage, and their move appeared to be a disaster. There had to be a Last Hurrah, and it had to be big.

Chapter 12

♣

A BRIDGE TOO FAR

A POPULAR 1977 MOVIE DRAMATIZED THE WORLD WAR II EXPLOITS of an allied military force that crossed the Rhine and destroyed a number of German-held bridges. On the last one, however, they were overwhelmed by superior Nazi forces. The closing scene was a discussion between two top officers, one of whom had opposed the operation as "a bridge too far"—the film's title. The year 1928 was one in which the Irish political machines stormed a bridge too far—possession of the Presidency itself.

It is not at all surprising that the attempt was made. Their strength in the Democratic Party was at an all-time high. Where they did not control the cities themselves, they controlled the machinery that selected convention delegates. The leaders had mastered the very fine art of making firm alliances with other ethnic groups by a careful rationing of the spoils of victory. The cities had expanded by leaps and bounds, creating more blue-collar jobs for men and, in the garment trades, women, which were filled by newly arrived immigrants. The Southern racists had diminished power and could no longer fight the Northerners to a draw. Finally, there was a candidate ready, willing, and able with an impressive record as a state legislator and governor of New York—Alfred Emanuel Smith.

Al Smith was the epitome of all the finest traits that had been developed by the Irish organizations since the Potato Famine. He was possessed of superb political skill; he was a first class orator; he had lifted himself out of the slums by his own bootstraps; his feelings for people in trouble ran deep; and he was scrupulously honest—as an expression of later years ran "hound's-tooth clean." These talents had been bent to honest administration of all his governmental jobs and to cleaning up Tammany. He was in the

[135]

tradition of Honest John Kelly and something of a thorn in the side of his organizational colleagues. The classic story involves an incident in which "the bhoys" were planning to run for office a man whose honesty had never been questioned because it did not exist. Smith was outraged and threatened to run against the man himself if Tammany put him on the ballot. One of the bosses present at the meeting challenged him as to what ticket he would use if he made the race. "I could run on a Chinese laundry ticket and beat that bum," he replied. The nomination was dropped.

To add to all of those virtues, Smith developed first a statewide and then a national outlook. The investigation that followed the Triangle Shirtwaist fire had made a deep impression on him. His childhood had been spent in desperate poverty—a situation which often leads men and women to greedy grasping at all the money that comes within their range. This was not the impact it made on Al. Instead, it left him with the profound conviction that something had to be done so people would be relieved from the kind of childhood he had experienced. His terms as governor of New York meant the strictest enforcement of protective legislation for men, women, and children workers—much of which he had succeeded, in company with Robert Wagner, in enacting into law when they were members of the State Assembly. They included regulation of sanitary conditions and elimination of fire hazards in factories, a state Workmen's Compensation Act, a "one-day-in-seven-rest" measure, and a Widowed Mother's Pension bill. He made New York the model for what might be called the economic protective state, even though it would be going too far to call it a welfare state, for Smith still thought in terms of people doing things for themselves. But he wanted everyone to have an equal chance at the starting gate and track judges to call foul when the rules were violated.

When one looks at the list of Smith's assets, he seems like the ideal Presidential candidate. Unfortunately for him—and for those who regarded him with affection and awe—he was also the embodiment, in most men's eyes, of the Irish machine politician and thus not a legitimate candidate for the White House. Smith's vision extended beyond the boundaries of New York City, but the eyes with which he viewed the rest of the world had first been opened on South Street near the Bowery. He had fallen just short of finishing the ninth grade in a parochial school and his real education came out of the Fulton Fish Market, where as a teenager he earned $12 a week rolling barrels of fish, icing them, wrapping them, and selling them. There is no doubt that he learned much about human beings on the job. But it made him inextricably a New Yorker. New York was not the whole United States, not even the prototype of the urban United States.

The friendships he had made as Democratic floor leader and Speaker of the New York State Assembly were strong and helped him make a successful race for the gubernatorial chair. But that was in a state which had a number of factory cities and factory small towns. It was a far cry from the rest of the country. Even in the Irish areas of Chicago, he looked peculiar to us. Our leaders did not dress that way, talk that way, or even walk that way. His accent was thick—not Irish thick but New York thick—and many of the things he said seemed to have no relevancy to our lives. He talked about issues like tariffs and water power, which meant nothing to Middle Westerners. And in Chicago, Prohibition was not much of an issue, because it did not prohibit anyone who wanted a drink from getting it, and it was not the symbol in the Windy City that it was in Gotham.

The most important qualification that Smith lacked can be stated very simply. In terms of the whole nation he simply was not contemporary. It would not be valid to describe him as a voice out of the past, but he certainly could not speak in the manner and tones of the heart of America in 1928. Even in terms of the Irish machines, he was becoming slightly passé. The sons and the grandsons of the Potato Famine immigrants were rising rapidly in American life. They were going to school and becoming lawyers and doctors and accountants. Al was like their fathers or their grandfathers—not exactly a greenhorn but with a sharp, ethnic edge. As for the other elements in the population, he was totally out of step.

Outside the ghettoes and the slums, a major obsession of the 1920s American middle class was the stock market. This had ceased to be an exclusive preserve for the wealthy and well-born. There were virtually no controls over margins in those days, and even blue-collar workers could buy fairly expensive securities with part of the baby's milk money. The Great Bull Market was in full sway, and the press appeared almost daily with predictions from leading economists (no one my age will ever have much confidence in economists) that it was going to rise much higher. People like my uncle—a blacksmith—were pouring lifetime savings into a market they did not understand in the slightest and were being fed, with great regularity, figures that demonstrated they were on Easy Street. No one with a personality antithetical to Wall Street had much of a chance with the nonethnic areas of urban America. Of course, the farmers were not enjoying prosperity in any form. But this was rarely mentioned in the press, and outside the South farmers were largely pro-Republican anyway. A Tammany leader from New York was hardly calculated to wean them from their traditional adherence to the party of Abraham Lincoln.

In retrospect, it seems incredible that the Democrats—not all of whom were tied to the Irish machines—should have cast their lot with Al Smith in 1928. Perhaps the nonmachine party leaders had a subconscious conviction that the party could not win anyway, so why not use the nomination as a reward for faithful service? Be that as it may, Smith was nominated on the first ballot of the Democratic Convention in Houston, Texas. For the first time in history, a Catholic—and, to make it more pointed, an Irish Catholic—received a nomination by a major political party to the highest office of the land. In just a little over three quarters of a century, the slogan "no Irish need apply" had been amended to make an exception for the White House.

For Smith, the good news of the nomination was about the last happy moment of 1928. What followed was a veritable firestorm of unabashed bigotry which has not been equaled in American politics in this century. Al and his followers had not been prepared for it. They did not understand the ignorance and narrowness of the fundamentalist mind and had assumed the religious issue could be resolved by discussion. In 1927, Smith had responded to an attack upon his Catholicism, which stated that he was disqualified as a President because he would have to give priority to his Church over the Constitution. In the response, he stated flatly that he believed in "the absolute separation of Church and State" and said that "I recognize no power in the institutions of my Church to interfere with the operations of the Constitution of the United States or the enforcement of the law of the land." It was not enough. The words were hailed as masterly by people who were already for him and greeted with disbelief by those who were not. Typical of the fundamentalist attitude was a statement by Bishop Adna Wright Leonard of the Methodist Church: "No governor who kisses the Papal ring can come within gunshot of the White House!"

In this kind of situation, a Fulton Fish Market education was of little avail. Smith was confronting fanatics, and fanatics spend all their time proving their beliefs whereas sensible people do not take every waking moment to disprove them. The nation was honeycombed with anti-Catholic ministers, who had spent years checking Papal bulls and pronunciamentos that had been moldering in musty libraries for centuries. One by one they were thrown at Al, who was completely helpless to answer because he had never heard of them. His religion was simple and direct, and he knew nothing about *Cur Deus Homo* or *Summa Theologica*. In his mind, the teachings of the Church were to "do justly, love mercy, and walk humbly with thy God." The long history of Catholicism as a temporal power was unknown to him.

At the public level, the religious aspects of the campaign were discussed in relatively intellectual terms. Below the surface, however, a word battle was raging unmatched in this century for virulence. By 1928, my family's status in the world had improved considerably, and we had moved to what sociologists call an "area of transition." This gave me many schoolmates who were not Catholic or Irish, and the playground talk, in retrospect, was raunchy. The story most repeated was that the Pope had selected "a nigger Cardinal" to move into the White House and take over the nation should Smith win. The Ku Klux Klan was literally flooding the nation with similar stories. And many people believed them— or at least claimed to believe them.

The real issue was probably not religion so much as the battle between the traditionalists and those who were trying to prepare for a new society. Basically, Smith and his advisers represented the ethnic groups in the cities battling for a grant of equal status with everyone else in American society. Many Americans were nervous over the thought that the wealth, acquired through the Great Bull Market, would somehow go away because of the actions of some "alien" leader who did not understand the United States. In their eyes, Smith was alien.

Smith did very little to calm the fears. He adopted as his campaign symbol the brown derby hat, which was associated in the minds of many Americans with street toughs and "wise guy" confidence men. (At one time members of the WHYOs, a savage set of New York Irish gangsters, adopted the derby hat as a type of helmet. It was hard weave and, stuffed with newspapers, could protect heads from heavy blows with cudgels. Other thugs took up the custom, and the meaning of the derby in the United States became quite different from that in England, where the bowler had an aristocratic aura.) Furthermore, Smith's pronunciation of certain words set him apart—the most memorable being "rad-ee-o" for radio.

Part of the uneasiness caused by Smith in financial circles should have been alleviated by his appointment of John J. Raskob, chairman of the board of General Motors, as his campaign manager. Raskob, although he had never had any previous political experience, was a man of great ability, but Smith handicapped him by concentrating on the very issues that were being used against him. He spent so much time attacking opponents for attacking him that the public had very little opportunity for judging him on any other issues. He had been warned that Oklahoma was a state where anti-Catholicism was notoriously strong and had been advised to soft-pedal the issue. Instead, he used his platform in Oklahoma City to center oratorical fire on the state's former senator, Robert L. Owen, who had refused to support Smith because of his Tammany affiliations. Smith scoffed at the "Tammany affiliations" statement and charged that it was merely a cover-up for religious bigotry.

First he spoke of Owen's "attempt . . . to inject bigotry, hatred, intolerance, and un-American sectarian division into a campaign which should be an intelligent debate on the issues which confront the American people." From there, he went on to excoriate the Grand Dragon of the Ku Klux Klan, a publication in Lexington, Kentucky, called the *Ashland Avenue Baptist*, and Mabel Walker Willebrandt, a Republican assistant attorney general, who had suggested to a Methodist convention in Ohio that they should use their numbers to swing the state against him. The basic themes of this speech were repeated all through the Middle West, where they would be the least popular and were varied only by attacks upon Prohibition—an issue where in 1928 he was a sure loser.

Under any circumstances, Smith would have had a great deal of difficulty beating his opponent—Herbert Clark Hoover, a man who had a great—and deserved—reputation as a humanitarian for his organization of Belgium food relief under Woodrow Wilson. Hoover was an engineer who had made a fortune through his own efforts and established himself as a hero with the business community during his term as Secretary of Commerce under Calvin Coolidge. He was the quintessential "pillar of society"—quiet, slightly pompous, and dressed like a captain of industry. His trademark was the high choke collar. He was a Quaker and presumably wedded to some form of pacifism, but Quakers were respectable people, and no one could see any war on the horizon in 1928. What counted was that no one could possibly picture Hoover as upsetting the stock market. As far as the electorate was concerned, he was a shoo-in, regardless of how Smith handled his campaign.

The election itself was a landslide. Hoover racked up 21 million votes compared to Smith's 15 million. What was much more devastating was that he carried only two Northern states—Massachusetts and Rhode Island—and had to cede four traditionally Democratic states of the old Confederacy to his opponent. Even New York State voted for Hoover—at the same time electing Democrat Franklin Delano Roosevelt as its governor. Some voices prematurely assigned the Democratic Party to oblivion and looked for an almost perpetual reign of the GOP.

There were, however, some peculiar signs which few people noticed at the time. The Democrats had increased their control over the urban centers. When it came to the bread-and-butter races, the organization was still intact in almost every major city. In New York, Chicago, Philadelphia, Kansas City, the metropolitan areas of northern New Jersey, the machines were still working smoothly. Their only failure had been to persuade the electorate to reach higher on the ballot than they normally reached.

Looking back, it is tempting to regard the 1928 election as the high-water mark of the Irish machines. They were not able to win it. But they had at least succeeded in nominating one of their own as a major candidate. The future was not going to see any national victories for the Honest John Kellys and the Alfred E. Smiths. A new type of politician was standing in the wings—among the Irish and the WASPs. The machines would retain power on a gradually diminishing basis for many years to come—they did not really flicker out until 1976, with the death of Richard Daley— the last of the great bosses. But from 1928 on, their strength would lie in a supporting role for a new type of Irish politician, coming from Harvard and Yale rather than the Fulton fish market.

The 1928 election battle was "a bridge too far." But it was a glorious way to go.

Chapter 13

♣

From PADDY *to* PATRICK

AN ANCIENT MAXIM OF TAOISM HOLDS THAT A VICTOR SHOULD go into immediate mourning because victory is the first step toward defeat. Unfortunately for the Republican Party, it did not count many Chinese in its advisory echelons. The 1928 Presidential triumph was regarded by the GOP as a complete endorsement of the laissez-faire policies of two GOP Presidents—Warren G. Harding and Calvin Coolidge. In the eyes of industry, Herbert C. Hoover loomed as a man with the same outlook as his predecessors but with considerably more demonstrated ability. After all, he had been a successful mining engineer in China, had made an honest fortune, and had organized Belgian war relief. He was not charismatic or even popular in the sense that Harding had been popular. But he was respectable and reassuring. No one could think of him as a wild man who might upset the course of Wall Street prosperity by impulsive action.

There were some signs of trouble on the horizon, however. First, the Democratic Party had actually emerged from the 1928 election with improved grass-roots strength; the decision of New Yorkers to embrace Republican Hoover as President and Democrat Roosevelt as governor in one gigantic, electoral hug summed up the underlying mood of the United States. Second, the GOP control of the White House rested on a prosperity that was very thin. It was based on mass ignoring of debt, a conviction that the market could only go higher, and on indifference toward the problems of production. A minor setback would be enough to send margin calls caroming through the financial districts, bankrupting people right and left. But these thoughts did not keep members of the Republican Party awake at night.

Another factor was not so obvious, even to the people most

[145]

directly affected. The political machines were broadening their base and picking up new allies. A new type of Irish leader was arising, who was welcome in the parlors of sophisticated society and could conduct the business of politics in other places than corner saloons. Perhaps he was the grandson or great-grandson of Potato Famine immigrants, or the son of a later immigrant— or an immigrant himself—who had come to the United States because it represented greater opportunity than was available in the Old Country. But even when he became part of the organization, he was much more an integral part of American culture than the earlier breed.

Typical of the new Irish boss was Edward J. Flynn, who ran the Bronx for Tammany. Flynn's father, born in Ireland, had actually received a degree from Trinity College in Dublin. He had little trouble establishing himself in the United States, and young Ed lived a comfortable life and received a legal education at Fordham University. He established a flourishing law practice in the Bronx and entered politics almost by accident. The organization needed a respectable Bronxite to run for the New York State Assembly, and Flynn agreed to fill the role—probably because he had become bored with life in the courts. He had natural political talent, and a few years later, Charles Murphy—the last of the really strong Tammany leaders—asked him to take over the Bronx. It was a choice that was to have a major impact upon political history, for in 1928 he met Franklin D. Roosevelt, and in a very short time became one of FDR's closest political associates and advisers.

Another exemplar of the trend could be found in Chicago in the person of Edward J. Kelly. One would have expected Kelly to behave in the classical style of the Irish ghetto politician. He had been born in the Back of the Yards district made famous by James T. Farrell in *Studs Lonigan* and had to start working full-time as a boy to help support his family. He was not even able to complete grammar school. But despite grinding poverty, he went through night school and wound up as chief engineer of the Sanitary District, one of the most important governmental jobs in the area.

In Chicago, the title "chief engineer" could not be taken as a certificate of proficiency in engineering. But there was much more to Ed Kelly than a title. He looked like the chairman of the board of a major manufacturing company, but he had none of the naiveté usually exhibited by businessmen in politics. He entered the political world dry behind the ears and became the first Irish politician to gather all the reins of Chicago power into his hands. While he was doing this, he was also cultivating friendships over the nation, including that of a man named Franklin Delano Roosevelt. Kelly and Flynn were the only two machine leaders who came to enjoy a personal relationship with the First Family, including Mrs. Roosevelt herself. They had the quality FDR appreciated most—quiet effectiveness.

On a younger level than Flynn and Kelly were Irishmen of a more intellectual cast who were making their way up that political ladder bypassing the machine route. They included the fabled Tommy "the Cork" Corcoran, of New Deal fame, and still later Patrick Moynihan, whom no one would ever call Paddy. These were individuals who were equally at home in the faculty lounges of Harvard and the meeting rooms of the Democratic National Committee. George Washington Plunkitt would not have recognized them as fellow Micks, and Honest John Kelly would have scratched his head in bewilderment over the question of where such men could have gotten such names. They were the precursors of the future—the older ones for Roosevelt and the younger for John F. Kennedy. They were willing to deal with the machine, but it was not their primary preoccupation. Their eyes were on Washington.

Another factor to take into account was the rise of non-Irish machines in some areas. This became very apparent in Chicago where Bohemia-born Anton J. Cermak took over the entire city. The Czechoslovakian population was not large, but it was highly disciplined, and its leaders were the ultimate in political sophistication. Cermak had mastered the most important lesson of American politics. In the United States a majority is merely an interlocking relationship of minorities, who can come together to gain specific goals. The Cermak technique was simply to convince all of the minorities that they would get a fair shake from him and from no one else. Well over a third of Chicago's population was either foreign born or black, and Cermak had something for all of them, including those represented by Adolph J. Sabath, who could not speak English. He was also very shrewd about appointing businessmen to advisory boards, where they could reap some prestige and at least have their say about local affairs. This did not automatically switch industrial leaders to the Democratic Party, but it did blunt the keener edge of their opposition.

The Cermak sweep was so complete that one of my memories of the year was a headline in a Chicago paper which read: "Cermak to Zintak to (some Czech name I cannot remember), and the Irish are all out." This variation on the old baseball chant of "Tinkers to Evers to Chance, and the bases are all out" was colorful, but it was very unfair. Actually there was a close relationship between Kelly, Pat Nash, chairman of the Cook County Democratic Committee, and Cermak. Furthermore, other ethnic groups were coming to the fore. The most important were the Jewish organizations, clustered around the garment workers' district, and the Poles. The latter were just beginning to organize, but they had sufficient influence for Chicago politicians to turn out at Humboldt Park on Kosciusko Day.

Something of the same process was going on in New York City, where Jewish groups were coming forward rapidly, and the Italians were beginning to produce leaders with whom the politicians were forced to reckon. The most interesting development, however, was the increasing prominence of Fiorello La Guardia, who was a *Republican*. Of course, his Republicanism was something he wore rather lightly, and no one would ever mistake him for Robert A. Taft. But La Guardia did have a knack for creating excitement that was akin to the flamboyance of Theodore Roosevelt, and he was a pugnacious politician perfectly willing to go to the mat with Tammany or any other group. Ultimately, he was to become the most complete in-charge leader since Boss Tweed, but he also put an end to Irish leadership in Manhattan. The Irish remained a force with which to deal, because they continued to control the police and fire departments, the subway motormen and the bus drivers. But those groups were not overly anxious to have their conationals in City Hall. La Guardia did just as well with them as would someone who could trace ancestry back to the Emerald Isle.

As is true of all social institutions, the old-fashioned Irish boss did not disappear overnight. In Kansas City, Tom Pendergast had built a machine that controlled not only his home town but Democratic politics in the whole state of Missouri. What made him unusual is that less than 6 percent of the population of Kansas City was foreign born and less than 10 percent black. In Jersey City, New Jersey, Frank Hague, an ex–prize fight manager who had entered politics almost by accident, came about as close to being an absolute dictator as any other American except Huey Long. On one occasion, when a reporter asked him how some of his tactics in muzzling opposition squared with the law, his response was "I am the law." When Norman Thomas, leader of the Socialist Party, attempted to hold a rally in Jersey City in 1938, Hague had Thomas arrested without citing any violation of law and banned further meetings. He regarded the Congress of Industrial Organizations as subversive and stated that its founder—John L. Lewis—was "window dressing" for the Communist Party.

At this point, it might be well to note that Hague was of a different stripe from most of his fellow "bosses." In addition to his greed—which was topped only by Tweed—he resorted to strong-arm tactics on a grand scale. His machine came close to producing a police state. He rose to power by the customary route of controlling and distributing favors to his constituents. But he did not hesitate to resort to force against anyone who threatened him.

It did not take very long after the defeat of Al Smith for the future of the Democratic Party to brighten—and brighten considerably. Within a year, the stock market took a spectacular plunge. By November 13, some $30 billion in the value of listed stocks had been wiped out, and the decline had not been halted. The shock was felt throughout the nation and was even punctuated by a few suicides of investors who, in public mythology, were jumping out of windows in wholesale lots. A typical bit of "black humor" of the period cautioned people to be careful about bodies hurtling to the sidewalk when walking in front of the New York Stock Exchange.

Far more ominous than the black humor was the rapid rise in unemployment. By January of 1930, it was on its way to the 4 million mark, despite assurances from President Hoover in his annual message to Congress that confidence had been "reestablished" in the economy of America. But aside from public works, road construction legislation, and the establishment of the Reconstruction Finance Corporation, which did not become effective until the Roosevelt administration, the President could do little to counter the Great Depression. The symbol of the day was the soup line and World War I veterans peddling apples at a nickel apiece, under a special license in the famed Chicago Loop. The best-known song of the era was "Brother, Can You Spare a Dime." Farm prices plunged so low that farmers began to dump their milk on the highways and burn their wheat. Hauling their products to market cost more than they could get back. The nation's largest insurance companies had invested heavily in farm mortgages, and there was a period when some of them owned huge chunks of the best agricultural property in the Middle West. It was of little use to them, they discovered after some foreclosures, since they could not find buyers. Often, their best bet was to leave the defaulting family on the property so at least it would be maintained.

The shock of the Depression very quickly turned to anger, and it was directed specifically at Hoover. Homeless men erected shanty villages out of cardboard boxes in every city in the United States and called them Hoovervilles. Country people, who were reduced to killing and eating woodchucks, called them Hoover hogs, and firing employees was called Hooverizing. Most of the conversation on the streets assumed that Mr. Hoover was enjoying the situation and literally gloried in accounts of starvation. His physical appearance did not serve him well in such times. What before the election had looked like calm responsibility began to look like callous indifference to suffering. It was illogical and unfair, and it was also politically potent. In the 1930 Congressional elections, the Democrats gained control of the House of Representatives and increased their numbers in the Senate by eight. The hairline majority of the Republicans in the so-called upper chamber held only because the Senate does not send more than one-third of its members to the hustings during an election year.

Nobody could possibly have enjoyed the Depression—not even the machine bosses, who were hoping to capture the Federal government because of it. But they would have been less than human if they had not laid plans for 1932 and looked forward eagerly to the next Democratic Party national convention. The big question was who would get the nomination, and here they split into two camps, Roosevelt and Smith. Their choices had little to do with the distinction between the new or the old breed of politician. They came through with some highly unlikely combinations. For example, Pendergast and Flynn were for Franklin Delano Roosevelt first, last, and always. Ed Kelly was also an FDR man, but during this period he was subordinate to Cermak, who was not quite sure which way the cat would jump so his organization had endorsed former Senator J. Hamilton Lewis as a favorite-son nominee. Hanging on to that decision past a crucial point in the 1932 convention turned out to be the biggest political mistake of Cermak's life. One non-Irish boss threw all his chips into the Roosevelt pot at the start. He was Edward Crump, the "foxy grandpa" of Memphis, Tennessee, politics, whose machine looked like an early Tammany whose members had been endowed with honey-chile and magnolia accents.

There was what seemed to be great support for another nomination of Al Smith. The strongest of his backers was Boss Hague, who not only endorsed Al but launched heated attacks against Roosevelt. His theme was that FDR could not carry a single state east of the Mississippi. A collection of Democrats who had seen Roosevelt carry New York State as governor in a Republican presidential year could not have been highly impressed by that argument. But Hague's control over the New Jersey delegation was impressive, and he had a strong ally in Senator David I. Walsh, who could swing Massachusetts—as he demonstrated in a primary campaign where Smith and FDR were pitted against each other. Tammany was also anti-Roosevelt because of an investigation of the organization by a group set up by FDR as governor.

An interesting sidelight on the Massachusetts situation centered on the role played by James Michael Curley. Despite the picture of him as an absolute dictator painted in the novel *The Last Hurrah*, he did not have complete control over Boston, let alone Massachusetts. Boston was a city which had never had a boss of bosses, like New York or later Chicago. Instead there were neighborhood organizations, of which Curley's was one. This gave him a needed base, but his election victories owed at least as much to his oratorical skills as it did to his organization. He reasoned in the early thirties that, by jumping on the Roosevelt bandwagon early, he could conceivably wind up in full control over Federal patronage in Boston. On the other hand, he had nothing to gain by a Smith victory, because of the close ties between Smith and Walsh. It was not bad reasoning. The only trouble was that he persuaded FDR to enter the Massachusetts preferential primary with the promise that he would deliver enough votes to guarantee success. Together with FDR's son James, he formed a National Roosevelt for President Club of Massachusetts, which not only campaigned in his home state but sent pleas for support to party leaders throughout the United States. The fabled Jim Farley, Roosevelt's ambassador to the Irish machines, and another trusted adviser, Louis Howe, cautioned against the ill-fated enterprise, but Roosevelt listened to Curley, and Walsh won with ease, handing all thirty-six state delegates to Smith.

There was an interesting aftermath to the Massachusetts debacle. After his election to the Presidency, FDR threw all his patronage to Walsh simply because he had demonstrated his ability to carry the state. Curley, who had beaten the pro-Roosevelt drums early, loud, and long, received nothing in exchange for his labors other than a couple of friendly letters and an occasional smile.

There was an even more interesting aftermath involving Hague. As soon as the convention ended, Hague was on the phone to Farley promising to produce "the largest political rally ever held in the United States" if FDR would open his Presidential campaign in New Jersey. Roosevelt, who knew that the state could not be carried without the help of the Jersey City boss, agreed and began his formal campaigning with a speech at Sea Girt before a crowd of 100,000 to 115,000. After that, Hague was "in" and, to the distress of many of the idealistic New Dealers, became one of the few "untouchables" in the nation. All—literally all—patronage was channeled his way, and naturally he repaid by delivering the state in election after election.

The years between 1928 and 1932 were mostly years of maneuver, and the Paddy's Pig type of Irish boss did not realize that he was gradually being eliminated from positions of real power. The final decision at the Democratic National convention was not their doing even though they had a hand in it. The delegates who arrived for the meeting were not of the old style—content to leave national affairs alone as long as they were left to rule over their cities. They wanted the White House, and they did not realize that what they were doing was to nominate a man who, once he became President, would hold the whip hand over them. In the future their position would rest on their relations with FDR, who would become the Boss of Bosses.

Chapter 14

♣

The BOSS *of* BOSSES

THE ROOSEVELT ERA WAS THE TRUE LAST HURRAH FOR THE IRISH machines. A few lingered on even after FDR passed away—especially in Chicago—but this was a winding-down process. It was not a painful demise, and the gradual descent into Limbo was graceful and left the members—outside of Tammany in New York City—with a sense of honorable passage. There were no tumbrels, no firing squads, no guillotines, but the inauguration of Franklin Delano Roosevelt diverted the course of history's mainstream, and the machines were not in it. They had become superfluous to American society, and the useful things that they once did were now being handled at a higher level than the neighborhood—or even the city or even the state. FDR's New Deal established Washington, D.C., as the focal point of the nation's life in peace as well as in war.

The transition to a Presidency-conscious country is difficult to comprehend for anyone who did not live before the change began. As a small boy, I was the only lad in my neighborhood who knew that Calvin Coolidge was President of the United States. My knowledge came from a motoring vacation to the East, which included a guided tour of the White House, where my mother was enchanted by a painting of Grace Coolidge in a red dress posed with a white collie dog. She talked about it all the way home, which, in those days, was a three- or four-day drive. It did not take me very long to discover that none of my schoolyard buddies cared in the slightest, and the adults merely gave me the kind of fatuous smile that grown-ups always shed when a brat comes up with what they consider an esoteric piece of knowledge. They knew who was president when they stopped to think about it. But who cared? Both the kids and the adults, however, could give you off the top of their heads the names of the mayor, many members of the City Council, the district attorney, the chief of police and the chief of detectives, the ward leader and most of the precinct captains. Those were "real" people, who had something to do with the way we lived. In school, of course, we heard about George Washington and Abraham Lincoln, whom we remembered chiefly because there were legal holidays named after them, which gave us some respite from classes. The older folks frequently mentioned Woodrow Wilson and Theodore Roosevelt, but that was because so many of them had served either in World War I or the Spanish-American War.

The change was virtually instantaneous. By the time I entered high school, everybody knew that Herbert Hoover was President and that somehow he had steered us into a sea of misery. At first blush, this seems unfair. But after all, Hoover and his Republican colleagues had accepted the credit for good times, and it was not surprising that they had to take the blame when the world in which we lived went sour. Perhaps Al Smith might have lost to Hoover in 1932, because he was still outside the mainstream of the United States. But it is doubtful that Roosevelt could have lost even if he had dropped dead before Election Day. The tide was running out.

The adulation with which Roosevelt was greeted was a clear signal that national government was here to stay. He never actually mastered the Depression, and full employment (or at least an approximation of full employment) did not come about until we entered the war in Europe. But he did give the voters their money's worth in action. During the first hundred days after his inauguration, Congress acceded to a hundred of his major requests. This was the famous rubber-stamp period, in which he could secure approval merely by sending something in writing to Capitol Hill. One of the principal criticisms of Hoover had been his failure to act. In reality, much of that was due to the balkiness of a Congress controlled by Democrats who saw happy days just ahead. But the voters were in no mood for carping. Many of the FDR measures were taken directly from some of Hoover's ideas. But again, who cared? The name on the laws—regardless of paternity—was Franklin Delano Roosevelt, and it was mighty in the land.

For many years, searching attempts were made by intellectuals to discover the theoretical basis of the New Deal. The young college graduates who surrounded Roosevelt in the White House fed out a steady stream of respectable academic names. At one period, the "in" intellectual was identified as John Maynard Keynes whose theories called for combating depressions with tax cuts and inflation with tax increases. At another point, Louis Bean and Mordecai Ezekiel were hailed as the men whose ideas were going to save American agriculture. Home-grown eggheads were brought directly into the government—or at least to the Rooseveltian councils. FDR early established what he called a Brain Trust which included such heavyweight thinkers as Raymond Moley, Adolf Berle, and Rexford Tugwell. Most of them deserted him after a few years or were relegated to obscure posts. Whether the leader of the New Deal paid much attention to them—aside from using them as window dressing—is very doubtful.

Seen from the distance of nearly half a century, Roosevelt looks simply like the most pragmatic President the nation ever had. Liberals embraced him heartily because they thought that the opposite of Harding, Coolidge, and Hoover had to be a liberal. But he was constantly driving them to despair by playing games with men like Hague, Flynn, and Kelly. The intellectual foundations of the New Deal were very simple. When there was a problem, do something about it, and do it with flair. He was not without ideals. He did want a prosperous United States, and he did want to preserve Western civilization from the Nazi barbarians. But he had no methodological approach to those goals. He merely wanted to know what would work and did not want to be bothered with abstractions or abstruse theories of society. He was exactly what the nation needed—a man who would not allow ideology to stand in the way of action.

The President was at his most pragmatic in dealing with the city machines. He used a political touchstone. If they could help him seize and exercise power, he would reciprocate with the kind of patronage that would keep them in power. If they became a liability or could not deliver the vote, they were cut off ruthlessly. Crump, Kelly, Flynn, and Hague flourished under the New Deal despite the anguished screams of the more idealistic Presidential aides. They *could* deliver the vote, they *would* deliver the vote, and they had enough sense not to stray too far from legality and get into the kind of trouble that would reflect upon the White House. Pendergast and Curley went down to defeat—the first because his corruption became too evident, and the second because he couldn't pull his weight on election day. In both cases, Roosevelt was ruthless, and both were cut off from federal patronage.

No city hall patronage could possibly compete with what FDR could make available. The New Deal created a host of organizations, which could put thousands of people to work in a few days' time. There was the WPA, which employed men and women on thousands of Federal projects from traffic surveys to construction of public facilities; there was the CCC, which took young Americans out on the land for soil conservation and reforestation; there was the NYA which held forth part-time jobs to needy college students; there was the PWA which supplied money for construction of dams and other major public works. Control over this rich flow of money and jobs was in the hands of Roosevelt's most trusted attendants, who, in turn, passed it out through state and city officials who could deliver the votes. The money went to people who needed it, and no one can argue that it was unnecessary. But the largesse very clearly came to people as the result of having Franklin D. Roosevelt in the White House. In turn, this meant that recipients liked to have Roosevelt's friends in control at the local level.

What is most remarkable about the whole process, however, is that none of the bosses really survived the New Deal. Most of them laid down their power voluntarily or died while still holding it. But they were not replaced! Except in Chicago, and to a lesser extent Pittsburgh, the boss system passed from our political life. It should be added that, in the exceptions, the bosses were forced to develop new methods of keeping themselves alive. Daley and Dave Lawrence in Pittsburgh actually ran efficient cities.

It is customary in many circles to adopt the theory that the demise of the bosses was caused by the New Deal creation of more efficient ways of handling the problems of poor people. This is an explanation that cannot be disregarded altogether. A WPA (Work Projects Administration) job was certainly preferable to a day's work shoveling snow or to walking through a park picking up scrap paper—about the best a member of the organization could offer to a down-and-outer. But the explanation is much too simple. There were deeper forces at play. Society was undergoing changes that made the boss not only unnecessary but possibly even a hindrance to progress. At the height of bossism, economic forces all through the society were focused on the local political leader for help in making the system work. The contractor thirsted for the construction projects of City Hall. Shopkeepers needed some "understanding" administration of the laws in order to survive. Even charitable projects had to have the appropriate blessing from the machine, or the money might not be forthcoming.

The important impact of the New Deal upon this system was that all of these economic and social chains-of-command were transferred to Washington. The Federal largesse, of course, was often dispensed at the local level, which enabled the boss to maintain some of his power. But he now held it as an agent for FDR, the Boss of Bosses. Furthermore, the conditions that had produced the individual Irish leader had also gone. Those men, and by now a few women, who were rising up through the political ranks were not rising as Celts but as Americans of Celtic descent. They could depend upon Irish votes as a question of sentimentality, but only to the same extent that an Italian could depend upon Italian votes or a German upon German votes.

Furthermore, men and women were grouping themselves together in other forms than political parties. There might be some ethnic ties in what they were doing. But the politics they played was usually secondary to their basic reason for coming together. In New York City, for example, one of the most important political forces centered around the garment trades unions—whose members had an unusually high degree of education and urban sophistication. They did form the American Liberal Party in the late 1940s, but its mission was to select candidates from both the Democratic and Republican parties so they could run on a Liberal ticket. The tradition of straight-ticket voting persisted even longer in New York City than it did south of the Mason-Dixon line. A "liberal" Republican might be attractive to large blocs of the city's Democrats, who could not bring themselves to vote for him under the GOP label. They could, however, vote for him under the Liberal Party banner.

One of the real straws in the wind is the fact that the Liberal Party was the creature of Alex Rose, head of the hat maker's union, and David Dubinsky, president of the International Ladies Garment Workers Union. They were not Irish, but they became the men with whom Presidential aspirants dealt when they were seeking either New York delegates to a Democratic convention or New York electoral votes the following November. The strength of their party persisted through Roosevelt, Truman, Eisenhower, Kennedy, and Johnson. Another straw in the wind was the disillusionment with FDR suffered by both Al Smith and Jim Farley, the first with roots deeply embedded in the Irish boss tradition of the past and the second in the early stages of the transition to the national scene. The New Deal tended to tilt more and more to intellectuals and academics as time went on. There was less and less room for the men from the streets.

As far as the Democratic Party itself was concerned, the city machines were taking a distinctly lower place to other types of organizations. Blue collar workers had generally voted Republican. But there were important changes in union organizations in the 1930s. Organized labor, spurred by John L. Lewis, president of the United Mine Workers, had launched a militant crusade in 1935 to unionize blue-collar workers on an industrial basis. This meant a political path into towns grouped around single industries, such as a steel mill or an electrical or textile plant. Traditionally, the small towns had been Republican in the North. Furthermore, the craft unions—carpenters, masons, plumbers, etc.—had also cast in their lot with the GOP, because of close ties with the contractors, which had led the two groups to work together in order to secure city ordinances favorable to construction.

In 1932, Roosevelt had received a heavy share of the blue-collar vote, but that was basically a function of the antagonism toward Hoover and large-scale unemployment. By 1936, the CIO, even though it was a young organization, had attracted men and women fired with the same enthusiasm that must have animated the crusaders who fought to rescue the Holy Grail from the infidels. Lewis's own resources were limited, and he assigned them almost exclusively to the steel industry, where organization was put under the charge of his top man, Phil Murray. There was plenty of voluntary help in organizing other industries, such as electrical, automobile, farm implement manufacturing, textiles, and rubber production. A radicalized generation of college youth (to save questions, I was one of them myself) leaped into the fray. Sophomores and juniors spent their weekends picketing local plants and passing out CIO leaflets at the gates of nearby factories. Unfortunately for the CIO in later years, some of them were young Communists (again to save questions, I was not one of these—my ties were to the young Socialists) who helped their older party members gain control of some of the unions simply by being in on the ground floor in the organizing process. In some instances, the hold became so strong that the CIO in later years, seeking to purge itself, was unable to shake the Communists loose and was forced to establish rival unions.

What is important about this development in a book exploring the Irish role in American politics is that most of the newly formed unions turned almost automatically to the Democratic Party. There were two basic reasons. The first was that the shock of the Great Depression had alienated so many of its traditional constituencies that the Republicans, outside rural New England, were dominated by the most reactionary type of industrialist. The second is that in the early stages of his administration, FDR launched the passage of legislation designed specifically to give unions extra clout in dealing with management. First there was Section 7A of the National Industrial Recovery Act, which awarded brownie points to corporations with good labor-management records. Second, there was the Wagner Labor Relations Act, which penalized legally definable unfair practices against union organization. With a record like that, where else could the new unions go?

There were many more votes available from organized labor than from the city machines. Furthermore, the ethnic groups that had supplied the strength for the Irish leaders could be reached even more easily through the United Steel Workers or the United Electrical Workers or the United Automobile Workers. Men like Hague and Kelly could not be disregarded, and in the intraparty maneuvering that resulted in the selection of delegates and candidates they were invaluable. But the keen edge was definitely gone. They were no longer the sine qua non of Democratic politics. There were still plenty of Irish-American politicians around, but they were no longer Irish-organization politicians. This was the period in which the road traveled by the Potato Famine immigrants and their descendants came to an end. The song was over even though the melody lingered on.

Some of the bosses, such as Kelly and Hague, remained potent through the Roosevelt administration and the Truman administration that followed. But most of them had sung their swan songs by the time Republican Dwight D. Eisenhower took over. In New York, Tammany was now being regarded with sentimentality, and the Hague machine in New Jersey could not be kept going after his retirement. Jack Kennedy attributed an important share of his Presidential victory in 1960 to Mayor Daley of Chicago. But in a sense the Chicago boss was summed up by Oliver Wendell Holmes's poem on "the last leaf upon the tree in the spring."

Even the gathering of political money became an operation directed out of Washington rather than ward headquarters. There was not only a new breed of political leader, but a new breed of businessmen who were quite willing to put money into the Democratic Party and Roosevelt without going through a boss. FDR early instituted a $100-a-plate dinner, where reasonably wealthy tycoons paid up to $1,000 a table for the privilege of gnawing at a leathery steak (and sometimes only chicken à la king) plus having their names on a list of party contributors that might give them an introduction to the White House somewhere down the line. In later years, the tab went to $1,000 a plate for both Kennedy and Johnson. With money like that coming in, who needed ward heelers for anything?

The Potato Famine immigrants had come to the United States fleeing English rule and looking for a square meal. In less than a century, they had run the full cycle so successfully that they had put themselves out of business. In the last analysis, it was irrelevancy, and not the reformers, that killed the Irish machines.

There was one final spasm from the Potato Famine immigrant, which resulted in the exposure of the darker side of the Irish soul. It came through the late Senator Joseph McCarthy, whose name has lived on as a synonym for irresponsible and malicious demagoguery. For a brief period of years—from 1949 to 1954—he ran a veritable reign of terror in the United States, and it took the combined forces of the Senate leadership in both parties to put an end to his career. It is one of the most astonishing chapters in our political history.

In the late 1940s, the American people were shocked by some investigations in the House of Representatives that demonstrated that secret Communists had infiltrated the government—some at fairly high levels. The damage that they did was minuscule, but when it was revealed that some minor points of atomic-bomb technology got to the Soviet Union through espionage channels, the public became alarmed. Had the whole thing ended when the more responsible investigations concluded, no harm would have been done, but unfortunately, the matter did not end at that point.

McCarthy, a man previously unknown outside his home state of Wisconsin, suddenly erupted with a blast of charges that the government—especially the State Department—was honeycombed with secret Communists who were known to, and presumably protected by, Secretary Dean Acheson. It became obvious almost immediately that McCarthy had no information whatsoever and probably could not locate a Communist on May Day in Moscow's Red Square. The press assumed that this would go away. It did not. McCarthy suddenly emerged as the most earth-shaking politician on the domestic scene. His followers swarmed into the Capitol in Washington, D.C., to pay homage to their hero. They cared nothing about facts and were totally impervious to arguments. What they sought was target identification. McCarthy's political strength reached a point where even Dwight D. Eisenhower, probably the most universally popular President of the twentieth century, hesitated to tangle with him.

The reason McCarthy belongs in this book lies in the improbability of his accusations. At the time, most people assumed that there was no rhyme or reason to what he was doing except making a few headlines. What they missed was the consistency of the type of person he named as Communist conspirator. Invariably, these people were members of an intellectual and aristocratic elite. His major target was Dean Acheson, Secretary of State in the Truman administration. Acheson was a man of rare diplomatic skill and, at the same time, probably the most hard-line anti-Communist in government circles. This attitude gave him no protection whatsoever. He was also cold in demeanor, aloof, icily intellectual, and afflicted with the facial expression of someone avoiding a foul smell. He had been one of the chief architects of the successful policy of containment launched by Truman, which McCarthy characterized as "Dean Acheson's cowardly school of communist containment." He also loved the phrase "the red Dean."

McCarthy tangled with Senators Saltonstall and Baldwin in the Senate and eventually lit upon a man named Owen Lattimore, a professor at Johns Hopkins University, as his chief Communist spy in the United States. This charge was absolutely ludicrous. Like many other intellectuals of the 1930s, Lattimore may have been attracted to some anti-Fascist causes. Furthermore, he had actually gone to China and interviewed Mao Tse-tung before the latter assumed power. But to label him as a major spy and an influence in the State Department (where he had never held an appointment) was silly. Nevertheless, the charges were believed.

Why were they believed? McCarthy's following was highly ethnic. It consisted of people who in the 1920s and much of the 1930s had suffered from a society that looked down upon them as Wops, Polacks, Dagos, Micks, Hunkies, and Heebs. What he was saying to all of them was "Hey, Giovanelli, Pilsudski, Pat, Jacob! You are the real Americans! It's those Achesons, Marshalls, Saltonstalls, and Lattimores who are Communist traitors." It was music to their ears.

I knew Joe well, and I doubt whether he really knew what he was doing. He was reacting instinctively to something that worked and that allowed him to take out his frustrations against the respectable world. The most revealing line about him was produced by columnist Mary McGrory, who wrote that anyone who had grown up where she had would recognize the type immediately— "the Irish bullyboy." She had described him precisely and also had nailed down the real reason for his "crusade."

Joe became intoxicated with power (and often with booze) and eventually found himself face to face with both liberals and conservatives in the Senate. He was censured by a heavy vote— unanimous among the Democrats, backed by half the Republicans. The censure broke his political back. My last view of him was that of a drunk shuffling down a street near the Capitol. He was closing out the dark side of the victims of the Famine

Chapter 15

♣

The AFTERGLOW

THE END OF THE MACHINE AGE DID NOT PUT AN END TO THE IRISH any more than the end of the open range put an end to the cowboy. There were Irish who continued to vote for Irish names out of sentimental reasons. There were Irish politicians who were Irish by descent but not by organization. Even Daley was finally knocked out by the reformers in the 1972 convention, but he was a very lonely man long before that happened.

Granting Daley all the credit or discredit he deserved for keeping the past alive after the funeral, the fact remains that the public image of the Irish politician changed long before his political demise. Up into the 1950s, the phrase evoked such names as Curley, Hague, Pendergast, and Kelly. But toward the end of the decade perceptions had shifted, and the names with which one could conjure were Kennedy and, a little later, Moynihan. Both of those men were indubitably Irish by descent. But it would take an incredible stretch of the imagination to classify them as walking in the footsteps of Croker, Pat Nash, or the O'Connells. They were not Irish-Americans but Americans of Irish descent. Even Woodrow Wilson would have been satisfied with their credentials.

Some Irish issues persist to this day, but they are not domestic issues—jobs for deserving Celts or construction contracts. Prohibition and the Ku Klux Klan disappeared during the era of Roosevelt, and although anti-Catholicism still is something of a force in the United States, its virulent forms have been reduced to small groups of fanatics caught up in abortion politics. What remains is the question of Ulster, which even today still divides Congress. One of the big battles on the floor of the House of Representatives in the spring of 1990 was an amendment for the foreign-aid bill, which would have restricted American contributions to the Inter-

[171]

national Monetary Fund until a General Accounting Office audit proved that the money was not being dispensed in a manner that discriminated against Catholics in Northern Ireland.

An interesting feature of the Ulster debate is that two successive House Speakers of Irish descent—Tip O'Neill and Tom Foley—have opposed such restrictions. Foley went so far as to lead the movement that deleted such an amendment from last year's foreign aid bill. He was roundly denounced for his action by the Ancient Order of Hibernians, whose spokesman described him as a "bridesmaid to the British." The language does not seem to have bothered the Speaker in the slightest. He, O'Neill, and Ted Kennedy belong to a different organization—the Friends of Ireland—whose moderate approach to the Ulster problem is probably much closer to the feelings of most Americans of Irish descent than the attitude of the AOH.

There are persistent rumors that arms and money still flow to the outlaw IRA from South Boston, Queens, and the Bronx. Leaders such as Ted Kennedy have cautioned against such aid, but they have done so on an "if it exists" basis. If it does exist it probably involves people who have a terrorist psychology and would find some other outlet if there were no conflict in Ulster. When I was a child in the early 1920s, Irish communities would and did shelter men smuggling illegal arms to Ireland. But today such behavior is not community activity.

Sometimes one wonders whether the issue is being kept alive out of a feeling of romanticism. The further Americans are from the Potato Famine, the more the Irish blend into the general population. At the same time, however, Irish publications are increasing rapidly. Magazines, newspapers, and leaflets fill the mails, and the American Conference on Irish Studies grinds out material by the yard. These are first-rate publications of scholarship, easily on a par with the works of classical literature. The question that pops into the mind is whether academics only form organizations to study a specific topic once it has become a part of our past.

The campaign for the Presidency of John F. Kennedy may

offer the best glimpse of modern reality. It was very definitely one that made use of but did not rest upon any Irish machine. JFK was surrounded by highly sophisticated assistants who were thoroughly conversant with the style of politicking in the 1960s and who did not waste their time chasing the phantasms of the past. Their targets were the Jewish organizations, the black organizations, the veterans of World War II, and the intellectuals. A friend of mine who taught at Harvard during the late 1950s gave me a picture of the campaign to win the allegiance of his colleagues at that venerable institution. It consisted of frequent and lengthy sessions with the candidate in the evenings, where he sought their advice (the most flattering act a politician can perform is to ask someone for guidance) and the distribution of token gifts—not expensive enough to cause resentment but tasteful enough to exact admiration.

The Kennedy tactics worked. They attracted men such as Arthur Schlesinger and John Kenneth Galbraith, who might have defended Al Smith against bigotry but would never have been enthusiastic about the prospects of a Smith administration. It established an image of Kennedy as a man who sought "the finest" and who loved brains—but who could offset any imputations of snobbery with his warm, outgoing personality. A Woodrow Wilson might have assembled similar supporters, but they would have made him appear aloof, with eyes fixed above the level of the common man. There was an air of brilliance to the Kennedy entourage, and it was the kind that appealed to his fellow Americans. The lack of a similar group behind him was one of the principal handicaps suffered by his only real opponent for the Democratic Presidential nomination in 1960—Lyndon B. Johnson.

Irish advisers such as Ken O'Donnell, Larry O'Brien, and Dave Powers served Kennedy with the traditional zeal and fierce devotion of clan members toward the leader, and they were probably closer to Kennedy than all the others. But their functions were not dealing with machine leaders. Instead they were directing campaigns that targeted quite different types of voters. They were seeking the Jewish vote, the labor vote, and the black vote. In doing so, they made intensive use of all the newly discovered polling techniques that have now become the bedrock of American politics.

It is doubtful whether the Catholic issue played much of a role in the campaign. In Houston, Texas, Kennedy faced an auditorium loaded with Protestant ministers and emerged from the confrontation in good shape. It would be going too far to claim that he made any votes in the process, but there is little doubt that he pulled whatever fangs were left in the issue. Al Smith had lived most of his life in a Roman Catholic environment and was totally unprepared for fundamentalist thinking. Kennedy's world had not been bound so completely by Irish neighborhoods, and he knew how to be graceful in religious arguments and how to conduct them without generating more heat. As a Johnson assistant (naturally we coordinated our efforts), I also had the feeling that there were some Americans who had a sense of shame over the kind of bigotry that surfaced in 1928 and who may have voted for JFK to prove they were not bigots themselves.

Whether Catholics voted for Kennedy because he was Catholic—or whether *all* Irish voted for Kennedy because he was Irish—is a question open to doubt. Older Irish and Catholics almost certainly cast their ballots for him. But there have been studies that suggest that younger people split their votes largely on the basis of economic status. The more affluent favored Nixon, the less affluent JFK. Exit polling techniques had not been highly developed in 1960, however, and I have never had any confidence in the studies I have seen.

Such questions are highly irrelevant when the 1960 election is surveyed overall. It was a close race because both men were of the World War II generation, and historically this was the year for that generation's assumption of power. The outcome was so close that forces that would have been minor in other elections became decisive. Had Dwight D. Eisenhower displayed some enthusiasm for Richard M. Nixon, who had been his Vice President, it might very well have led to a different outcome. If Kennedy had selected a different running mate than Johnson, he could very well have lost enough Southern states (where Nixon was basically more popular) to come in second in the electoral vote. And if Dick Daley had not delivered such a whopping margin in Chicago, JFK would have lost the decisive state of Illinois. Nixon wanted to contest the Illinois results, but President Eisenhower cut off the budding protest by recognizing Kennedy as the winner and immediately inviting him to confer at the White House.

In terms of the basic policies of the United States, the 1960 election cannot be considered a watershed. Kennedy, as President, carried on about the same policies that were advocated by his predecessors. The Alianza para el Progreso (Alliance for Progress) in Latin America did not differ from the Marshall Plan of Truman in Europe except that it did not produce as much in terms of concrete results. The disastrous invasion of Cuba at the Bay of Pigs had been planned and prepared in the Eisenhower administration, and all JFK had to do was to give the go-ahead. The nuclear test ban treaty had been cooking for many years and was the outcome of negotiations and study that had been started earlier. The Cuban missile crisis was handled well, and Kennedy proved both his guts and his political acumen when he stared the Soviets down. None of this was a change in policy—merely the reaction to events from the outside world. About the only enduring achievement of his administration was the Peace Corps, a quiet entity that is encountered only by those who stray off the beaten tourist paths in Third World countries and now in Eastern Europe.

From a political standpoint, however, the 1960 election was a turning point. It put an end to any lingering feelings of the Irish that they were strangers in an alien land. It also laid the groundwork for bringing the South back into full partnership with the rest of the United States. From the outbreak of the Civil War to the 1960 election, it had been understood that the Southerners were "out of it" where races for the presidency were concerned. Woodrow Wilson had been born in Virginia but was regarded by everyone as a New Jerseyite. He was definitely not grits, ham gravy, and black-eyed peas. John Nance Garner, of Texas, had achieved the Vice Presidency because Roosevelt needed the delegates from his state in the 1932 convention. He actually spent eight years in the Vice President's Capitol Office, where he poured a glass of bourbon for friends at the close of each working day. He visited the White House less often than the Senate Democratic and Republican leaders, and when people began to worry about FDR's health, he was quickly replaced.

The Southern plight was due basically to the region's devotion to racism. This did not mean that the rest of the United States was a model of tolerance—in fact many blacks found that their lives were even harder in Northern areas than they had been in Dixie. But in clinging to their segregation principles, the descendants of the Confederacy had sacrificed the fluidity that a society must have if it is to keep step with changing times. They had voted for politicians who promised them they would maintain their right to force blacks to the back of the bus. The image of the South that was presented to other Americans was that of the "hookworm and pellagra" belt. For them the play *Tobacco Road* summed up the South.

The image broke down to some extent with Lyndon B. Johnson—partly because he was from Texas, which Northerners are wont to associate with cowboys and oil rather than Simon Legree. In the post–World War II era, it was regarded as the least Southern of the Southern states. In addition, Johnson's roots were in the Texas hill country, which traces its history back to the War of Independence from Mexico rather than to the War Between the States. With that kind of base, he was not forced to be blatant about racism as he might have been had he represented other areas. Above all, however, he had amassed a highly liberal record as a Democratic leader of the Senate—a record that included education, medical and housing legislation, and the first Civil Rights bill enacted since 1875. In addition to that, he had been the first to recognize the potentialities of outer space and had sponsored the legislation that created the National Aeronautics and Space Agency.

The record was enough for him to receive the nomination for the Vice Presidency. It was not enough for him in 1960 to be nominated for the Presidency, but it did place him in a position to tour the nation and in general inspire in people a feeling of confidence that he could be trusted with power. His most successful appearance was before the Liberal Party in New York, where he brought an audience composed almost entirely of Jewish garment workers to their feet, cheering and screaming in virtual ecstasy as he left the hall. My most enduring memory of that day was hearing a newspaperman, who was bitterly anti-Johnson before the meeting, muttering to a colleague: "I certainly underestimated this show!"

What is important here is that the 1960 election left the nation more united (or more homogenized—pick your modifier) than it had been before. There were still "outsiders"—blacks, Latin Americans, Indians—but regional, religious, and ethnic lines had become blurred and in many instances disappeared altogether. Before 1960, the election to the Presidency of a Texan such as Johnson was highly improbable, and the election of a Georgian such as Jimmy Carter was unthinkable. Those conditions are now behind us. We have entered a new world, and the old one is not going to come back.

What may be even more significant is that since 1960, we have even begun to construct a form of politics that eliminates the organizational politician as well as the machine politician. In 1960, there were many targets for politicking—cotton growers, manufacturers, brokers, labor unions, manufacturers associations, the NAACP, teachers' associations, and others. Today, most politicking ignores those groups in terms of their formal structure. None of them can deliver votes except possibly the NAACP, which represents one of the few segments of our society that is excluded from full participation because of who their members are rather than what they do. Even among blacks, some changes are becoming noticeable as more and more of them get elected to higher and higher office. A black governor of Virginia at one time could have existed only in a liberal's wildest fantasy. Today it is an actuality. Furthermore, there has been a slight increase in the numbers of blacks voting Republican in recent years, and my black students tell me that, while their parents are still solidly Democratic, they have a tendency to be either Republican or uninterested.

The disaffection with political organizations has gone far on both sides. Democrats have discovered that they can no longer count on a solid union vote, although organized labor still provides most of the Jimmy Higgins workers for Democratic campaign committees. At the same time, farmers in New England have tended to increase their Democratic votes to a point where Maine, New Hampshire, and Vermont—once the "rock-ribbed" areas of Republicanism—have loaded their State Houses with Democrats. In the modern world, no area and no economic class can be regarded as safely in the hip pocket of either of our major parties. The modern politician still shoots for classes of voters. But the major target has become the so-called middle class which must be reached on an individual basis.

Modern campaigning has become almost entirely a matter of television. It is doubtful whether any political leader can put on the kind of demonstration that the old machines could manage. No one who was there will ever forget Lyndon Johnson's 1964 parade in Chicago, where Daley had put everything he had into the scene. Block after block the procession wound past solid columns of men and women standing at rigid attention with the number of their ward and the name of the ward leader imprinted on huge signs held over their heads. Daley could tell at a glance who had delivered and who had not. The modern campaigner does not shoot for the demonstration but for the "sound bite." Speeches are planned and timed in order to hit the evening news shows with a few pithy words, and the visuals are just as important as what is said. During the last campaign, George Bush made a speech at a West Coast shipyard. The written press reported a hostile crowd. But the major impression of the American people as to what happened was that Bush, in his shirt sleeves, was being chummy with a group of workingmen. His actual "issue" campaigning consisted of commercials showing men walking in and out of a prison in a continuous line. It was a much more effective way of saying that his opponent was "soft on crime" than making a speech upon the subject. His opponent did not fully understand the "sound bite" system of politics, and his campaign was doomed from the start.

Of course, television costs big bucks—not just to buy the space but to hire all of the needed technicians. What this means is that most organizational campaigning these days is aimed at the PACs (the political action committees) which are the major sources for money. Where we were once concerned about the "undue influence" of political machines, we are now concerned about the "undue influence" of economic interests that can raise the money. All that can truly be said at this point is that American democracy is never free from worry and woe.

Chapter 16

♣

JUDGMENT DAY

WERE THE POTATO FAMINE IRISH MERELY A FREAKISH NOTE IN American history? Were they just another ethnic group who sought sanctuary in the United States and blended into the population? Was the passing of their political organizations a boon to American democracy and have we cleaned out all of the evil with which they were associated? Or is it possible that they fulfilled an historic role and left behind them enduring institutions?

There can be an answer to these questions either way without violating logic, and each response is arguable. If one eliminates as oddballs the few men of scrupulous integrity such as Al Smith and Honest John Kelly, the record is shot through with thievery on a major scale. Sometimes it was an activity performed with a degree of charm by such men as George Washington Plunkitt, with his distinction between honest and dishonest forms of graft. Sometimes it was performed with an unsavory odor of slavering greed by the members of the Tweed Ring. Sometimes it produced frightening arrogance as in the example of Boss "I am the law" Hague. Regardless of the coloration, however, it was still the illegal pilfering of the taxpayer's money in a clear circumvention of the laws that governed our society. Within the confines of Tammany and the machines of Boston, Chicago, Philadelphia, et al., there were only two definitions of ethical conduct that were taken seriously. One was that most of the Irish leaders were faithful to their wives. The other was that members of the machine would stick together when somebody blew the whistle on them. The word "morality" did not extend to the administration of the public trust.

The graft, however, was not the whole story. Did the Irish machines perform any services for the people of the cities? Here, regardless of how one feels about the chicanery of the bosses, the answer must be yes. At the very least they were a source of refuge for the poor who had no place else to turn. They quite literally performed social services that went beyond the limits of the poor house and the soup kitchens of religious denominations. They provided jobs for desperately hungry men, helping hands for bewildered immigrants, advocacy intervention with authority for helpless ghetto inhabitants who ran afoul of laws they did not understand. That does not excuse the chicanery. But when reformers raise that point, they should observe that no one else was performing such services. Respectable society was warm in its denunciations of the bosses. But its heart was not very warm when it came to dealing with the hungry and the dispossessed.

What is probably more to the point, would the melting pot really have melted if it had not been for the Irish? They led the way in integration of an alien culture to our country. Would another group coming over at the time—the Germans, for example—have done the same? Perhaps. But here we must consider an imponderable factor—the Irish character. For centuries they had been living under foreign rule. In the course of that process, they had acquired an amazing ability to slip through the cracks of the law. They had learned how to obfuscate, how to find elbow room, how to turn aside the wrath of soldiers who controlled fire power. In the United States, they found a parallel to what had happened to them in Ireland. It was true that the laws had not been deliberately framed to keep them down. It was also true that America's police and military forces had goals other than keeping the Irish in subjection. Nevertheless, the economic system was well developed, and it afforded no apparent route for penetration by the Potato Famine immigrants. It took ingenuity and craft to carve out a place in the sun under such circumstances while avoiding too much confrontation. In Italy and Eastern Europe—the two areas besides Ireland that supplied most of our conspicuous immigrants in the nineteenth and early twentieth centuries—these skills had not been highly developed.

One other point that must be considered is the crucial need of the American political system for unifying forces. The division of powers doctrine worked well in a simpler era, where government had little or nothing to do in terms of the daily lives of its citizens. If it was impossible to get together on programs, no one really cared too much. There was plenty of time after a stalemate to work out new proposals, and it was unlikely that anyone would be hurt by such a delay.

There is an old Hegelian principle that changes in quantity bring about changes in quality. Nowhere is this better illustrated than in the history of our cities in the last half of the nineteenth century. As the cities continued to grow, they changed not only in terms of size but in terms of what the population needed. In the early part of the nineteenth century, there was little or no need for police forces of size or groups of full-time firemen. A felon was unlikely to get very far with nefarious schemes simply because the routes out of town were too inefficient to permit fast getaways. Most householders were armed and knew how to shoot, and a stranger in the area would be marked and watched almost as soon as he came in sight. As for fires, those could be handled by bucket brigades.

The large metropolitan areas changed the situation. Not only did the realities call for police and fire forces, they also called for central administrations that were not bogged down in ideological disputes over money and interest rates. The Irish were suited to this situation. Aside from hatred of England, they carried no intellectual baggage. They had gone into politics to get a square meal, and their only real interest in government was jobs. They were willing to do whatever they needed to do in order to keep those jobs and that meant taking care of their constituents. Patronage may not be a very noble unifying force. But when one examines America's political history with care, it has been more effective than any other.

The key point to the whole equation is the timing. The Irish Potato Famine immigrants arrived here just as opportunity was opening up. It was at the very bottom of the ladder—the digging of ditches, the laying of railroad tracks, the guarding of other people's property against fire and theft. It was far from an affluent life, but it was much more affluent than anything they had known in their motherland. Furthermore, the railroad tracks and the factories represented the future, as did the rapidly growing cities. They were at the initial point of a wave that was destined to change all of Western civilization.

Is anything left of the institutions that the immigrants sponsored? That is a very difficult question to answer. One who has spent two years researching the Irish diaspora—and who is of Irish descent himself—has a strong tendency to attribute everything good in our political life to the Irish. Furthermore, we must allow for the fact that we do not know, and cannot know, what would be here today had history arranged itself differently. Taking all these factors into account, however, it is possible to discern certain features of our political life that at least parallel the boss machines.

First, there is the extreme pragmatism of American politics. This has been the despair of reformers and idealists for well over a century. Our political campaigns do not turn on economic or social issues. They hinge on voter estimates of the character and general philosophical leanings of the candidates. In a recent discussion at the University of Chicago, one of the students expressed indignation over the demise of the Presidential campaign of Senator Gary Hart of Colorado. Hart was well known in Washington, D.C., for a roving eye. Some of the stories about his escapades were so well known that he was questioned about them. His response was that the press should follow him and find out for itself. One newspaper took him up on the challenge, and he led them into a love nest. That was the end of Gary Hart as a Presidential candidate. The indignant student cited a series of economic proposals that Hart had advanced in speeches and said that voter judgment should have been based on those proposals rather than on Hart's personal life.

Another student immediately challenged the assumption. He said that Hart's action had demonstrated that "the man is either stupid or suicidal, and I do not believe that either condition is a qualification for the Presidency."

The second student was expressing the basic viewpoint of the Irish politician. The candidates should be judged on character rather than on speeches. The Irish love speeches and have produced some great orators, such as James Michael Curley. But when it comes to decisions on leadership, they looked for the telltale signs of character, which will emerge when a man's personal life is examined. In my judgment, Eisenhower defeated Stevenson because he appeared to be more of a "solid citizen," and Kennedy defeated Nixon because he looked more trustworthy. It took a national crisis to put Nixon in the White House.

Equally important, however, is the concept that the government has an obligation to help individual citizens when they are in trouble. This very definitely was the thrust of the Irish machines. One wonders whether Franklin D. Roosevelt himself would have been so anxious to establish a direct linkage between the Presidency and people in trouble if it had not been for his early associations with Al Smith and his lasting friendship with Ed Kelly and Ed Flynn. His Brain Trust presented him with programs to carry out his goals, but the basic desire to do so went back to the Triangle Shirtwaist fire and the association with Smith. The older school of national leadership thought of "the people" as a mythic entity. To Theodore Roosevelt the nation's wilderness was to be preserved because it was the heritage of "the people." It would never have occurred to him to devote equal fervor to finding jobs for "the people" who were on their uppers in a depression.

Most important of all, however, was the concept of government as a "make a deal" process. It is impossible to spend any amount of time in the halls of our nation's capital without realizing that politicians had codified the Art of the Deal long before Donald Trump was even a gleam in his father's right eye. What comes out of Washington is the result of a give-and-take process in which all interested parties sacrifice some of their demands in order to get what they really need and find themselves supporting some of what they have opposed, because there is no other way to win anything. Reformers who view the process find it abhorrent. But there is

[187]

probably no other way to operate in a divided powers government. The notorious instability of so many Latin American governments is almost certainly the outcome of a divided powers constitution without a tradition of compromise. There were Irish in Latin America too, but even though they rose to high positions (after all, the first President of Chile was Bernardo O'Higgins) they could not overcome the Spanish tradition, fostered by the long years of Moorish occupation, that politics is a clash between angels and devils in which the angels are entitled to obliterate the devils. Latin America became a morass of brutal oligarchies. *El Caudillo* was the only unifying force.

On one occasion, when I was the director of the Senate Democratic Policy Committee, I was assigned a political science professor as an intern. One day he came to me and said: "You know, George! I came here with all kinds of ideas as to what these men should do. I thought they needed more and better staff, that they should spend more time studying the issues in order to determine the best course of action. What I have learned is that these men come to the Senate with certain things that they have to do, and no amount of staff or time for reflection is going to make any difference. It is still going to come down to a deal. All the staffs can do for them is to feed them ammunition. It may be possible to improve the quality of the agreements. But it will still come down to the deal."

That is as good a note as any to close this book. We have learned how to handle democratic government by making a deal. The Irish were the first to practice this method as an everyday reality in political life. Perhaps someone else would have introduced it as if they had not been present. But they were on the spot.

The machines were marked by many unpleasant features. Their history is no model for how people should proceed in life. Today, some of the conditions that were partially responsible for the existence of the machines are still in effect. We have minorities in the United States who are still on the short end of the stick— notably blacks. Unfortunately, other conditions are gone. Society does not have the open cracks that greeted the refugees in the late 1840s and early 1850s. This means that blacks have had to resort to confrontation and to help from the law to get anything even approaching a fair deal.

The story is still worth studying. Perhaps we can find in it some guidance for handling problems of assimilation in the future.

APPENDIX

To the political reformers of the late nineteenth and early twentieth centuries, the Irish machines were evil forces against which all honest and patriotic Americans should rally. The result was the publication of muckraking articles that spluttered with indignation, exposed corruption in city governments, and did virtually nothing to unseat the bosses. There was one exception—an article by Jane Addams, the famous founder of Hull House in Chicago, who spent a decade fighting with Johnny Powers, who ruled the 19th Ward. She won some and lost some but in the course of her battles, she learned to appreciate the reasons why cities were run the way they were.

In April 1898, she published an article in The International Journal of Ethics *(now known as* Ethics *and published by the University of Chicago Press) summarizing the conclusions she, a contemporary antagonist who was capable of looking at both sides of the question, had reached. A portion of this influential piece appeared that same year in* The Outlook, *a sociopolitical magazine. This version is reprinted here.*

Appendix

Why the Ward Boss Rules

Primitive people, such as the South Italian peasants who live in the Nineteenth Ward, deep down in their hearts admire nothing so much as the good man. The successful candidate must be a good man according to the standards of his constituents. He must not attempt to hold up a morality beyond them, nor must he attempt to reform or change the standard. If he believes what they believe, and does what they are all cherishing a secret ambition to do, he will dazzle them by his success and win their confidence. Anyone who has lived among poorer people cannot fail to be impressed with their constant kindness to each other; that unfailing response to the needs and distresses of their neighbors, even when in danger of bankruptcy themselves. This is their reward for living in the midst of poverty. They have constant opportunities for self-sacrifice and generosity, to which, as a rule, they respond. A man stands by his friend when he gets too drunk to take care of himself, when he loses his wife or child, when he is evicted for non-payment of rent, when he is arrested for a petty crime. It seems to such a man entirely fitting that his Alderman should do the same thing on a larger scale—that he should help a constituent out of trouble just because he is in trouble, irrespective of the justice involved.

The Alderman, therefore, bails out his constituents when they are arrested, or says a good word to the police justice when they appear before him for trial; uses his "pull" with the magistrate when they are likely to be fined for a civil misdemeanor, or sees what he can do to "fix up matters" with the State's attorney when the charge is really a serious one.

Because of simple friendliness, the Alderman is expected to pay rent for the hard-pressed tenant when no rent is forthcoming, to find jobs when work is hard to get, to procure and divide among his constituents all the places which he can seize from the City Hall. The Alderman of the Nineteenth Ward at one time made the proud boast that he had two thousand six hundred people in his ward upon the public pay-roll. This of course, included day-

[192]

laborers, but each one felt under distinct obligations to him for getting the job done.

If we recollect, further, that the franchise-seeking companies pay respectful heed to the applicants backed by the Alderman, the question of voting for the successful man becomes as much an industrial as a political one. An Italian laborer wants a job more than anything else, and quite simply votes for the man who promises him one.

The Alderman may himself be quite sincere in his acts of kindness. In certain stages of moral evolution, a man is incapable of unselfish action the results of which will not benefit some one of his acquaintances; still more, of conduct that does not aim to assist any individual whatsoever; and it is a long step in moral progress to appreciate the work done by the individual for the community.

The Alderman gives presents at weddings and christenings. He seizes these days of family festivities for making friends. It is easiest to reach people in the holiday mood of expansive good will, but on their side it seems natural and kindly that he should do it. The Alderman procures passes from the railroads when his constituents wish to visit friends or to attend the funerals of distant relatives; he buys tickets galore for benefit entertainments given for a widow or a consumptive in peculiar distress; he contributes to prizes which are awarded to the handsomest lady or the most popular man. At a church bazaar, for instance, the Alderman finds the stage all set for his dramatic performance. When others are spending pennies he is spending dollars. Where anxious relatives are canvassing to secure votes for the two most beautiful children who are being voted upon, he recklessly buys votes from both sides, and laughingly declines to say which one he likes the best, buying off the young lady who is persistently determined to find out, with five dollars for the flower bazaar, the posies, of course, to be sent to the sick of the parish. The moral atmosphere of a bazaar suits him exactly. He murmurs many times, "Never mind; the money all goes to the poor," or "It is all straight enough if the church gets it."

There is something archaic in a community of simple people

in their attitude towards death and burial. Nothing so easy to collect money for as a funeral. If the Alderman seizes upon festivities for expressions of his good will, much more does he seize upon periods of sorrow. At a funeral he has the double advantage of ministering to a genuine craving for comfort and solace, and at the same time of assisting at an important social function.

In addition to this, there is among the poor, who have few social occasions, a great desire for a well-arranged funeral, the grade of which almost determines their social standing in the neighborhood. The Alderman saves the very poorest of his constituents from that awful horror of burial by the county; he provides carriages for the poor, who otherwise could not have them; for the more prosperous he sends extra carriages, so that they may invite more friends and have a longer procession; for the most prosperous of all there will be probably only a large "flower-piece." It may be too much to say that all the relatives and friends who ride in the carriages provided by the Alderman's bounty vote for him, but they are certainly influenced by his kindness, and talk of his virtues during the long hours of the ride back and forth from the suburban cemetery. A man who would ask at such a time where all this money comes from would be considered sinister. Many a man at such a time has formulated a lenient judgment of political corruption and has heard kindly speeches which he has remembered on election day. "Ah, well, he has a big Irish heart. He is good to the widow and the fatherless." "He knows the poor better than the big guns who are always about talking civil service and reform."

Indeed, what headway can the notion of civic purity, of honesty of administration, make against this big manifestation of human friendliness, this stalking survival of village kindness? The notions of the civic reformer are negative and impotent before it. The reformers give themselves over largely to criticisms of the present state of affairs, to writing and talking of what the future must be; but their goodness is not dramatic; it is not even concrete and human.

Such an Alderman will keep a standing account with an undertaker, and telephone every week, and sometimes more than once, the kind of outfit he wishes provided for a bereaved constituent, until the sum may roll up into hundreds a year. Such a man understands what the people want and ministers just as truly to a great human need as the musician or the artist does. I recall an attempt to substitute what we might call a later standard.

A delicate little child was deserted in the Hull House nursery. An investigation showed that it had been born ten days previously in the Cook County Hospital, but no trace could be found of the unfortunate mother. The little thing lived for several weeks, and then, in spite of every care, died. We decided to have it buried by the county, and the wagon was to arrive by eleven o'clock. About nine o'clock in the morning the rumor of this awful deed reached the neighbors. A half-dozen of them came, in a very excited state of mind, to protest. They took up a collection out of their poverty with which to defray a funeral. We were then comparatively new in the neighborhood. We did not realize that we were really shocking a genuine moral sentiment of the community. In our crudeness, we instanced the care and tenderness which had been expended upon the little creature while it was alive; that it had every attention from a skilled physician and trained nurse; we even intimated that the excited members of the group had not taken part in this and that it now lay with us to decide that the child should be buried, as it had been born, at the county's expense. It is doubtful whether Hull House has ever done anything which injured it so deeply in the minds of some of its neighbors. We were only forgiven by the most indulgent on the ground that we were spinsters and could not know a mother's heart. No one born and reared in the community could possibly have made a mistake like that. No one who had studied the ethical standards with any care could have bungled so completely.

Last Christmas our Alderman distributed six tons of turkeys, and four or more tons of ducks and geese; but each luckless biped was handed out either by himself or one of his friends with a "Merry Christmas." Inevitably, some families got three or four apiece, but what of that? He had none of the nagging rules of the charitable societies, nor was he ready to declare that, because a man wanted two turkeys for Christmas, he was a scoundrel, who should never be allowed to eat turkey again.

The Alderman's wisdom was again displayed in procuring from down-town friends the sum of three thousand dollars where with to uniform and equip a boys' temperance brigade which had been formed in the ward a few months before his campaign. Is it strange that the good leader, whose heart was filled with innocent pride as he looked upon these promising young scions of virtue, should decline to enter into a reform campaign?

The question does, of course, occur to many minds. Where does the money come from with which to dramatize so successfully? The more primitive people accept the truthful statement of its sources without any shock to their moral sense. To their simple minds he gets it "from the rich," and so long as he again gives it out to the poor, as a true Robin Hood, with open hand, they have no objections to offer. Their ethics are quite honestly those of the merry-making foresters. The next less primitive people of the vicinage are quite willing to admit that he leads "the gang" in the City Council, and sells out the city franchises; that he makes deals with the franchise-seeking companies; that he guarantees to steer dubious measures through the Council, for which he demands liberal pay; that he is, in short, a successful boodler. But when there is intellect enough to get this point of view, there is also enough to make the contention that this is universally done; that all the Aldermen do it more or less successfully, but that the Alderman of the Nineteenth Ward is unique in being so generous; that such a state of affairs is to be deplored, of course, but that is the way business is run, and we are fortunate when a kind-hearted man who is close to the people gets a large share of the boodle; that he serves these franchised companies who employ men in the building and construction of their enterprises, and that they are bound in return to give jobs to his constituency. Even when they are intelligent enough to complete the circle, and to see that the money comes, not from the pockets of the companies' agents, but from the street-car fares of people like themselves, it almost seems as if they would rather pay two cents more each time they ride than give up the consciousness that they have a big, warm-hearted friend at court who will stand by them in an emergency. The sense of just dealing comes apparently much later than the desire for protection and kindness. The Alderman is really elected because he is a good friend and neighbor.

During a campaign a year and a half ago, when a reform league put up a candidate against our corrupt Alderman, and when Hull House worked hard to rally the moral sentiment of the ward in favor of the new man, we encountered another and unexpected difficulty. Finding that it was hard to secure enough local speakers of the moral tone which we desired, we imported orators from other parts of the town, from the "better element," so to speak. Suddenly we heard it rumored on all sides that, while the money and speakers for the reform candidate were coming from the swells, the money which was backing our corrupt Alderman also came from a swell source; it was rumored that the president of a street-car combination, for whom he performed constant offices in the City Council, was ready to back him to the extent of fifty thousand dollars; that he, too, was a good man, and sat in high places; that he had recently given a large sum of money to an educational institution, and was, therefore, as philanthropic, not to say good and upright, as any man in town; that our Alderman had the sanction of the highest authorities, and that the lecturers who were talking against corruption, and the selling and buying of franchises, were only the cranks, and not the solid business men who had developed and built up Chicago.

All parts of the community are bound together in ethical development. If the so-called more enlightened members of the community accept public gifts from the man who buys up the Council, and the so-called less enlightened members accept individual gifts from the man who sells out the Council, we surely must take our punishment together.

Another curious experience during that campaign was the difference of standards between the imported speakers and the audience. One man, high in the council of the "better element," one evening used as an example of the philanthropic politician an Alderman of the vicinity, recently dead, who was devotedly loved and mourned by his constituents. When the audience caught the familiar name in the midst of the platitudes, they brightened up wonderfully. But, as the speaker went on, they first looked puzzled, then astounded, and gradually their astonishment turned to indignation. The speaker, all unconscious of the situation, went on, imagining, perhaps, that he was addressing his usual audience, and totally unaware that he was perpetrating an outrage upon the finest feelings of the people who were sitting before him. He certainly succeeded in irrevocably injuring the chances of the candidate for whom he was speaking. The speaker's standard of ethics was upright dealing in positions of public trust. The standard of ethics held by his audience was, being good to the poor and speaking gently of the dead. If he considered them corrupt and illiterate voters, they quite honestly held him a blackguard.

If we would hold to our political democracy, some pains must be taken to keep on common ground in our human experiences, and to some solidarity in our ethical conceptions. And if we discover that men of low ideals and corrupt practices are forming popular political standards simply because such men stand by and for and with the people, then nothing remains but to obtain a like sense of identification before we can hope to modify ethical standards.

Jane Addams
Hull House, Chicago

BIBLIOGRAPHY

General Irish History

Foster, R. F. *Modern Ireland, 1600–1972.* London: The Penguin Press, 1988. A scholarly and lucid history of Ireland, which begins with the Norman invasion, chronicles the spread of English control and the disaster of the Potato Famine, and describes the homeland whose existence was a unifying factor for the American Irish.

Kee, Robert. *Ireland.* Boston: Little, Brown and Company, 1980. A kaleidoscopic view of Irish history from 8000 B.C. to modern times, in which a conscientious attempt has been made to separate historical fact from historical fiction. Valuable as an overview.

Lyons, F. S. L. *Ireland Since the Famine.* New York: Charles Scribner's Sons, 1971. A scholarly appraisal of Irish history from 1850 to the present era, which is valuable because of the interaction between the American-Irish and the Irish-Irish, which had such a vital impact on both nations.

MacManus, Seumas. *The Story of the Irish Race.* Rev. ed., Old Greenwich, Conn.: The Devin-Adair Company, 1921. A highly romanticized history of Ireland, which is still basically valid. It should be read to capture the mood of Irish writers in the early part of the twentieth century (and also for the rich language, which is akin to the musical arts).

O'Faolain, Sean. *The Irish.* Old Greenwich, Conn.: The Devin-Adair Company, 1949. An effort by one of Ireland's best-known writers to trace the history of Irish thought and the factors that went into the Irish ethos.

The American Irish

Asbury, Herbert. *The Gangs of New York.* Garden City, N.Y.: Garden City Publishing Co., Inc., 1927. This is a lurid and readable account of the formation of New York City gangs—mostly Irish—beginning in the early and mid-nineteenth century. The account is lopsided but historically valid, and it paints the gangsters in the shades in which they were regarded by their contemporaries.

Broehl, Wayne. *The Molly Maguires.* Cambridge, Mass.: Harvard University Press, 1963. An effort to separate fact from fiction on the Molly Maguire organizations—named after secret societies in Ireland—that operated in the Pennsylvania coal regions in the nineteenth century.

Clark, Dennis. *Hibernia America.* Westport, Conn.: Greenwood Press, 1986. This is an exploration of the spread of the Irish in the United States from the seaport cities along the Atlantic Coast across the continent and up into Alaska. This book is an excellent guide to the differing Irish cultures that arose at different points on the map.

Cuddy, Joseph Edward. *Irish-America and National Isolationism, 1914–1920.* New York: Arno Press, 1976. This book was submitted as a doctoral dissertation to the State University of New York at Buffalo. But it was such a thorough analysis of the contest between Irish hatred of England and Irish love for the United States (in which the United States won) over the issue of participation in World War I that it was published by the Arno Press. It is well worth reading as a guide to the transition of Irish thought in America.

Greeley, Andrew. *That Most Distressful Nation: The Taming of the*

American Irish. Chicago: Quadrangle, 1972. A picture of the Irish community that exists in the United States today.

McCaffrey, Lawrence J. *The Irish Diaspora in America.*Washington, D.C.: Catholic University of America Press, 1976. This book by the noted American-Irish scholar is the best short explanation of the Irish experience in America. It is virtually a "must" for those interested in the subject.

Miller, Kerby A. *Emigrants and Exiles: The Irish Exodus to North America from Colonial Times to the First World War.* Berkeley, Calif.: University of California, 1976. An excellent work on the conditions and development of the Irish in the United States.

Shannon, William V. *The American Irish*. New York: The Macmillan Company, 1963. This is *the* classic on the American Irish—a timeless book that is worth reading over and over again by anyone interested in the development of the American-Irish enclave.

Woodham-Smith, Cecil. *The Great Hunger*. New York: Harper & Row, 1962. This is probably—and deservedly—the most widely read account of the Potato Famine that launched the Irish diaspora.

The Irish-American Politician

Brownell, Blaine A. and Warren E. Stickle, eds. *Bosses and Reformers*. Boston: Houghton Mifflin, 1973. This is a collection of essays by American political scholars on the bosses and their opponents. Thoroughly researched and presented in scholarly style to scholars, it is still good reading for anyone who is interested in politics but not particularly in political science.

Dedmon, Emmett. *Fabulous Chicago*. New York: Random House, 1953. An entertaining but historically valid account of the workings of Chicago's political machines. The author was one of that city's most distinguished journalists.

Dorsett, Lyle. *Franklin D. Roosevelt and the City Bosses*. Port Washington, N.Y.: Kennikat Press, 1973. This book explores the relationship of Franklin D. Roosevelt to the bosses. The author disputes the thesis that the New Deal ended bossism but does not give much consideration to the alternative thesis: that the New Deal may have set in motion forces that put an end to bossism after FDR left the political scene. This is an excellent account of the period when city machines could actually determine the outcome of elections.

Erie, Steven P. *Rainbow's End.* Los Angeles: University of California Press, 1988. This is a carefully researched book on the history of the Irish political machines. The author faults the Irish bosses for not using their power constructively.

Granger, Bill and Lori Granger. *Lords of the Last Machine.* New York: Random House, 1953. A well-researched history of the various Chicago machines and the factors that would ultimately lead to their demise. The book, written by a husband-wife team, combines academic and journalistic experience.

O'Connor, Edwin. *The Last Hurrah.* Boston: Little, Brown & Company, 1956. Although this is a novel, rather than a scholarly study, O'Connor captures the spirit of the Irish politician better than anyone else who has tried to do so. The book should be read simply because the Irish machines cannot be understood solely by a quantitative and chronological study.

Riordan, William L. *Plunkitt of Tammany Hall.* New York: Alfred A. Knopf, 1948. This charming, but brief, book is a collection of discourses by George Washington Plunkitt, perhaps the most colorful of all the Irish politicians, which he delivered over the years from his "throne"—a shoeshine stand in City Hall. Riordan acted as an amanuensis. It is not only entertaining but presents superb insights into the philosophy and psychology of the Irish boss.

Robinson, Frank S. *Machine Politics.* New Brunswick, N.J.: Transaction Books, 1977. This is what might be termed a "cameo study" of the political machine established by the O'Connells in Albany, N.Y. Students of the process believe a persuasive argument can be made that it was the most efficient ever established.

Walsh, James P., ed. *The Irish: America's Political Class.* New York: Arno Press, 1976. A collection of essays on the rise of Irish political machines, which focuses heavily upon the reaction of contemporaries to them. Should be read for an understanding of the interaction between the Irish and the non-Irish in the United States.

American Economic Development

Davis, Lance E., Richard A. Easterlin, and William V. Parker. *American Economic Growth: An Economists' History of the United States.* New York: Harper & Row, 1977. Davis, Easterlin, and Parker formed a committee that solicited manuscripts from the leading economists of the United States. The result is a book that has become a standard reference for economic historians.

United States Department of Commerce, Bureau of the Census. *Historical Statistics of the United States: Colonial Times to 1970.* U.S. Government Printing Office. This is regarded as the most reliable source of statistical information on our nation.

General

Allen, Frederick Lewis. *Only Yesterday, An Informal History of the Nineteen-Twenties,* New York: Harper Bros., 1931. This book is more effective than any other I know in conveying the bewildering sense of change in this decade.

Burns, James MacGregor. *Roosevelt, the Lion and the Fox.* New York: Harcourt Brace, 1956. This book is an excellent overview of the manner in which President Roosevelt was able to play off various political forces in our society.

Jones, Maldwyn A., "*Emigration*" in *Encyclopedia of American Economic History.* New York: Scribners, 1980, vol. 3.

Reeves, Thomas C. *The Life and Times of Joe McCarthy.* New York: Stein and Day, 1982. This is a carefully researched book by a noted historian on the last gasp of the Irish revenge against respectable society.

Terkel, Studs. *Hard Times; An Oral History of the Great Depression.* New York: Pantheon Books, 1970. Affords a compelling view of life during the depression.

INDEX

Acheson, Dean, 165–67
Act of Union (1800), 25
Adams, John Quincy, 87
Addams, Jane, 68, 69–70, 78–79, 191
Albany, New York, 64, 66, 88, 93, 129
Amalgamated Clothing Workers, 82
"America First" slogan, 128
American Conference on Irish Studies, 8, 172
American Irish, The (Shannon), 26
American Liberal Party, 162
Ancient Order of Hibernians, 172
Anglo-Irish, the, 10, 17, 37
Anglo-Irish Treaty of 1921, 106
Anglophobia of Irish, 1–5, 10–22, 31, 91, 103, 127–28
anti-Catholicism, in U.S., 27, 40, 67, 89, 113–14, 138–41, 171
anti-immigrant attitudes, 36, 113, 115
anti-Irish attitudes, in U.S., 6–7, 36, 47, 113; waning, 107
anti-Semitism, 114
Armagh, County, 20
Asbury, Herbert, 46
Ashland Avenue Baptist, 141
assembly-line production, 112, 126
Awful Disclosures of the Hotel Dieu in Montreal (book), 40

Baldwin, Senator, 166
ballot-box stuffing, 63, 80–81, 84, 92

Baptist church, 113
Barn Burners, 36
Barry, John, 37, 103
baseball, 7–8
Bauler, Paddy, 129
Bean, Louis, 159
Belmont, August, 67
Benton, Thomas Hart, 35
Berle, Adolf, 159
Berlin, Irving, 126
Beyond the Melting Pot (Moynihan), 47, 62
blacks, 11, 30, 31, 38, 45, 65, 114, 176–77, 188–89; vote, 173, 177–78
boodlery, 31, 82–84, 130; see also graft
bootlegging, 113
bossism, 65–71, 75–81, 82–84, 89, 90, 91–93, 129–30, 146–47, 149, 160–61; decline of, 142, 160–61, 164–65; see also machine politics
Boston, 28; Irish, 8, 28, 41, 75–76, 89–90, 104, 152, 183; population figures, 42, 63, 76; Yankees, 89–90
Bowery Boys, 45
boxing, 7, 8–9, 65, 104
Brain Trusts: FDR, 159, 162, 187; JFK, 173
Braunfels von Solms, Prince Otto Karl, 38–39
Brennan, John, 90
Brennan, Matthew, 65

Index

Brian Boru, 16
Brice, Fanny, 126
British rule over Ireland, 16, 17–22, 30, 40, 47; Act of Union (1800), 25; Anglo-Irish Treaty of 1921, 106; resistance to, 18–19, 20–22, 25
Brooklyn, New York, 93
Bryan, William Jennings, 93, 95, 114–15, 119
Buchanan, James, 36
Buckley, Christopher A. "Blind Boss," 75, 93, 130
Buffalo, New York, 64, 88, 93
Bush, George, 178
business, Republican Party and, 52–53, 54, 94, 130, 163
Butler, Pierce, 37
Butte, Montana, 64

Calhoun, John, 35
campaign funds, 164–65, 179
Canada, Irish migration through, 25, 64, 89
Cantor, Eddie, 126
Capone, Al, 92
Carter, Jimmy, 177
Case–McAllister Committee, 83
Catholic Church, in U.S., 114, 139; Irish domination of, 40, 48
Catholicism, as presidential election issue, 138–41, 174
Celts, 12, 19, 28
Cermak, Anton J., 91, 147–48, 151
Chicago, 77, 90–91, 137, 178; DA's office, 9, 129; ethnic groups, 91–92, 127–28, 147–48; 1st Ward, 81, 92, 129; Irish in, 3–5, 8–9, 28, 41, 64, 88–89, 90, 92–93, 104, 127, 128–29, 183; Irish in control of, 68–70, 75, 91, 127, 146–47, 152, 157; 19th Ward, 68–70, 79, 191, 192–98; patronage jobs, 61, 68, 89, 160; population figures, 42; survival of boss system and machine under Daley, 142, 157, 160–61, 164; vote fraud, 80, 81
Chicago Tribune, 6, 81, 128
Christianity in Ireland, 15–16, 21–22
Cincinnati, 93
CIO (Congress of Industrial Organizations), 82, 149, 163
cities, big, 36, 54–55; Democratic control of, 53–54, 94, 119, 123, 129–30, 142; Democratic vs. Republican, 93; demographic figures, 42, 63, 124; franchise selling, 79, 196–97; growth,

28, 36–37, 39, 42, 54, 95–96, 111, 124, 127, 135; Irish in, 8, 28–29, 39–42, 63, 87–93; Irish in control of, 7, 40, 59–63, 65–71, 87, 88–93, 123, 127, 128–30, 135; passing of boss system, 157, 160–61; payrolls, 61, 83, 89, 95–96; public works contracts, 66, 77, 83, 96; regulatory functions, 61, 80; role in social change, 39–40, 123–24
Civil War, 51; draft riots, 28, 45–46
clan system, Irish, 16–17, 18–19, 27, 41, 48
Clay, Henry, 35
Cleveland, Grover, 53, 94
coal industry, 6, 28, 37, 64
Cokran, Bourke, 114
Colby, Bainbridge, 118
Collins, Dan, 4
Communists, 149, 163, 165–66
community cohesiveness, Irish, 27, 30, 41, 47–48
Confessions of a Nun, The (book), 6
Congress, 11, 54, 94, 102, 158, 171; see also House of Representatives; Senate
Connolly, Richard B. "Slippery Dick," 65, 88
Conscience Whigs, 36
constituent service, 67–68, 78–79, 184, 192–96
Constitution, U.S., 11, 37
construction trades, 28, 29, 65, 81, 88–89, 96, 161, 163, 185–86
Cook County Democratic Committee, 68, 148
Coolidge, Calvin, 111, 127, 141, 145, 157, 159
Corbett, "Gentleman" Jim, 7, 104
Corcoran, Tommy "the Cork," 19, 147
corruption, 88, 160; see also graft
Coughlin, "Bathhouse John," 81, 92, 129
Cox, George, 93
Cox, James, 115, 116–17, 124
Croker, Richard, 71, 87, 88, 171
Crump, Edward, 151, 160
Cunniff, Michael M., 90
Curley, James Michael, 62, 75–76, 90, 152, 160, 171, 187
Czech-Americans, 68, 80, 91, 127, 147–48

Daley, Richard J., 3, 41, 91, 142, 161, 164, 171, 175, 178
Davis, John W., 116–17
Dead Rabbits, 45

[206]

Index

Debs, Eugene, 115
democracy, 63; Jacksonian, 35
Democratic Party, 51–55, 93–95, 102, 106, 111–19, 149; antebellum split, 36, 106; as Irish base, 53–55, 65, 88, 93, 123–24, 135; labor and, 53–54, 162–64, 178; local urban base, 53–54, 93, 94, 119, 129–30, 142, 162; 1924 national convention, 116–19, 123, 124; 1928 national convention, 138; 1932 national convention, 151–53; in North, 51, 53, 93, 106, 111, 115–19, 178; in presidential elections, 53, 93–94, 95, 106, 111, 112, 114–19, 124, 138–42, 145, 151–53, 172–77; in South, 52, 53, 93, 106, 115–19, 123, 124, 135; in state politics, 111, 142, 145, 178; voter base changes, 162–64, 178
Derry, County, 20
De Sapio, Carmine, 65
Dewey, John, 131
diaspora, Irish, 19, 25, 42, 186
Doherty, Michael, 90
Donegal, County, 20
Dubinsky, Dave, 82, 162
Dublin, 17, 22, 37, 89, 104
Dunne, Finley Peter, 8, 104
Dunne, George, 90
Dwyre, "Doc," 6

Eastern European immigrants, 30, 31, 68, 80, 113, 115, 184
Egan, Mike, 4
Eisenhower, Dwight D., 162, 164, 166, 174–75, 187
elections, 31, 53, 79–81; black vote, 177–78; farm vote, 52, 53, 54, 95, 138,178; labor as factor in, 54, 162–64, 178; machine politics, 63, 179 (see also vote buying; vote fraud); middle class vote, 54, 178; PACs' role, 179; post-Civil War South, 52; presidential, 11, 53, 93–94, 95, 102, 106, 111, 112, 114–19, 131, 138–42, 145, 151–53, 172–79
Elizabeth I, Queen of England, 17–19
Emmet, Robert, 21
Emmet, Thomas Addis, 26
Erwin, Andrew D., 118–19
ethnic groups, 80, 103, 127–28; cooperation vs. rivalry among, 31–32, 50–51, 63, 91–92, 135, 147–48; and McCarthyism, 167; national vote, 164
Evans, Hiram, 114
Ezekiel, Mordecai, 159

factory system, 28, 35, 37
Farley, James, 152–53, 162
Farmer-Labor Party, 95
farmers, 112, 138, 150; and Republican Party, 52, 53, 54, 95, 138, 178
Farrell, James T., 8, 146
favoritism, 79–80, 82–83, 149
favor trading, 51, 59–62, 76–77, 92, 105
Fighting 69th infantry regiment, 105
Fillmore, Millard, 36
Firbolgs, 19
fire departments: growth of, 28–29, 95; Irish control of, 7, 29, 50, 59, 65, 76, 89, 149
Fitzgerald, F. Scott, 107, 130
Fitzgerald, John F., "Honey Fitz," 75, 90
Fitzmaurice, Walter, 6
Fitzsimmons, Thomas, 37
Flynn, Edward J., 146, 147, 151, 159–60, 187
Foley, Tom, 172
Fomorians, 15, 19
Ford, Henry, 112, 116, 126
Friends of Ireland, 172
fundamentalism, 113–14, 115–16, 124, 139, 174

Gaelic invasion of Ireland, 15
Galbraith, John Kenneth, 173
Gangs of New York, The (Asbury), 46
gangsterism, 45, 91; Chicago, 91–92; Irish, 28, 29, 45–47, 91–92, 140; Italian, 92
Gargan, Thomas, 90
Garner, John Nance, 175
German-Americans, 63, 91, 92, 103
German immigrants, 30, 38
Gilbert, Danny "Tubbo," 129
Glazer, Nathan, 47
Gold Rush of 1850s, 64
graft, political machines, 65–66, 71, 77, 79, 82–84, 88, 149, 160, 183, 196; "honest," 68, 82, 83, 183
Grand Army of the Republic, 52, 94
Great Depression, 129, 150–51, 158, 163
Great Hunger, The (Woodham-Smith), 26
Greeley, Andrew, 8
Greeley, Horace, 39, 92, 93
Gregory, Lady Augusta, 4, 9, 10
guerrilla warfare, Irish, 18, 22
Guevara, Che, 19

Hague, Frank, 83, 129, 149, 151–52, 153, 159–60, 164, 171, 183
Harding, Warren G., 111, 115, 145, 159

Index

Harriman, Averell, 130
Hart, Gary, 186
Hat, Cap, and Millinery Workers, 82
Heflin, Tom, 114
Hemingway, Ernest, 130
Henry II, King of England, 15, 16
Henry VIII, King of England, 17, 19
Hillman, Sidney, 82
Hispanics, 31, 45, 65, 177
History of Tammany Hall, The (Connable and Silberfarb), 65
Hogg, Jim, 124
Holmes, Oliver Wendell, 164
"honest graft," 68, 82, 83, 183
Hoover, Herbert C., 111, 141–42, 145, 150, 158, 159, 163
House of Representatives, 11, 151, 165; Irish in, 26, 67, 171–72
Howe, Louis, 152
Hughes, Archbishop John Joseph, 46
Hull House, 68, 79, 195, 197
"hyphenates," 103, 104, 128

immigrants, immigration, 12, 30–32, 38, 42, 53–54, 63, 95, 113, 135; as power base of bosses, 63, 68, 78, 95, 115, 184; power base lost, 161, 164; restrictions on, 115; see also Irish immigrants
industrialization, 28–30, 35, 37, 42, 95; post-Civil War, 52–54
industrial unions, 81–82, 162–64
Industrial Workers of the World (IWW), 64, 94
industry, 54, 95, 112; cooperation with political machines, 77–78, 80
intellectuals, Irish, 9, 137, 147; see also Brain Trusts
International Journal of Ethics, 69–70, 191
International Ladies Garment Workers, 82, 162
Ireland, history of, 10, 15–22, 25, 30, 106; British rule, 16, 17–22, 30, 40, 47; potato famine, 25–26; Ulster debate of present, 171–72
Irish-Americans, 103–5, 106–7, 137, 161, 171; urban population, 63
Irish character, 22, 184
Irish consciousness, emergence of, 18, 19, 41, 47
Irish Ethos, 12, 30, 47–48, 76–77, 183, 198
Irish immigrants, 21, 25, 26, 63, 68, 113, 146; attempted bans on, 7, 36; Potato

Famine, 3, 5, 7, 9, 12, 25, 26–30, 37–42, 45, 55, 63–64, 165, 184–86
Irish Republican Army, 4, 64, 172
Italian-Americans, 63, 68, 80, 91, 92, 103, 148–49, 161
Italian immigrants, 30, 31, 68, 113, 184

Jackson, Andrew, 11, 35, 60, 87
Japanese-Americans, 104
Jefferson, Thomas, 87
Jersey City, 83, 92, 129, 149
Jewish immigrants, 30, 31, 63
Jews, 68, 92, 126, 127, 148, 173
Johnson, Hiram, 129–30
Johnson, Lyndon B., 19, 162, 165, 173–74, 176; 1964 campaign, 178

Kansas City, 75, 83, 92, 142, 149
Kelly, Edward J., 75, 91, 129, 146–47, 148, 151, 159–60, 164, 187
Kelly, "Honest John," 66, 70, 76, 83, 87, 88, 136, 142, 147, 171, 183
Kelly, Mike, 8
Kenna, "Hinky-Dink," 81, 92–93, 129
Kennedy, Edward M., 90, 172
Kennedy, John F., 8, 90, 147, 162, 164, 165; 1960 candidacy, 172–75, 187; as president, 175
Kennedy family, 90, 171
Kern, John W., 102
Keynes, John Maynard, 159
kickbacks, 77, 96
Kilkenny Parliament (1366), 17
Knights of Labor, 64, 94
Know-Nothings, 6–7, 36, 67
Ku Klux Klan, 106, 113, 114, 116–19, 123, 127, 140, 171

labor: and Democratic Party, 53–54, 162–64, 178; voting patterns, 54, 162–64, 173, 178; see also unions
labor laws, 53, 101, 136, 163–64
LaFollette, Robert, 112
La Guardia, Fiorello, 148–49
landlord-tenant system, Irish, 20–22
Last Hurrah, The (O'Connor), 63, 152
Latin America, Irish in, 19, 25, 188
Latin Americans, 31, 45, 65, 177
Lattimore, Owen, 166–67
law, Irish approach to, 27, 30, 47–48, 50–51, 61–62, 76–77, 83, 184
Lawrence, David, 129, 161
Lehman, Herbert, 130
Leonard, Bishop Adna Wright, 139
"leverage" positions, 76

[208]

Index

Lewis, J. Hamilton, 151
Lewis, John L., 149, 162, 163
Lewis, Sinclair, 130
Liberal Party, 162, 177
liberal politics, 159, 162, 176–77; Irish and, 101–2, 105–6, 118, 130
Limerick lawyers, 27, 30; Alibi, 27
Lincoln, Abraham, 52, 138
Lippmann, Walter, 130
local politics, 53–55, 93, 94, 127–30; see also cities; machine politics
Loco Focos, 36
Lomasney, Martin, 49, 90
Long, Huey, 149
Lumpenproletariat, 45–47

McAdoo, William Gibbs, 116–18
McCabe, Patrick, 93, 129
McCarthy, Joseph, 165–67
McCarthy, "Pinhead," 130
McCormack, John W., 90
McCormick, Robert R., 128
McDonald, Mike, 90
McGrory, Mary, 167
machine politics, 32, 51, 95–96, 100–1, 103, 107, 129, 179; beginnings of, 55, 87–89; decline of, 142, 153, 157, 162–64; demise of, 3, 142, 157, 160–61, 164–65; heritage of, 184–89; immigrant constituency of, 63, 68, 78, 95, 115, 135, 184; immigrant base lost, 161, 164; Irish, 26, 28, 32, 60–63, 65–71, 75–84, 87, 88–92, 94, 106, 107, 123, 124, 127, 129–30, 135, 142, 146–49, 157, 191; lack of social agenda, 62, 69, 95–96, 105; local orientation, 53–54, 93, 94, 123, 142; national arena, 106, 111, 116–19, 123–24, 135–42, 151–53, 162–64; non-Irish, 147–48; power, 63–66, 75–77, 79–80, 82, 96; power consolidation of 1920s, 123, 124, 127–30, 131; protective services, 7, 59–60, 61, 76, 83, 185; Roosevelt and, 152–53, 157, 159–61; social services void filled by, 60, 63, 67, 78, 95–96, 183–84, 192–96; see also bossism; favoritism; favor trading; graft; patronage; vote buying; vote fraud
McKay, Patrick, 26
McLaughlin, Hugh, 93
MacMahon, Marshal, 19
McManes, James, 93
Macmurrough, Dermot, King of Leinster, 16

McNair, William, 129
McTige, Mike, 8–9
Magee, Chris, 93
Maguire, Patrick, 90
Malloy, Father Pat, 4, 5, 6
Marx, Karl, 45, 47
mass transportation, 65, 88, 95, 100
melting pot, 31–32, 184
Methodist church, 139, 141
middle class, 138; vote of, 54, 178
Milesians (Sons of the Mil), 10, 15, 19, 37
Moley, Raymond, 159
Molly Maguires, 6, 64
Montgomery, Richard, 37
Moore, Edmund H., 118
Moynihan, Daniel Patrick, 47, 49, 62, 147, 171
muckrakers, 62, 130, 191
Murphy, Charles F., 71, 87, 88, 101, 146
Murray, Phil, 163

NAACP (National Association for the Advancement of Colored People), 177
Nash, Pat, 75, 91, 129, 148, 171
Nast (Thomas) cartoons, 47, 66
National Industrial Recovery Act, 164
National Labor Relations Act, 164
national politics, 52–53, 54, 93–94, 106, 111–19, 145, 151–53; entry of Irish into, 102, 106, 119, 123–24, 135–42; 1960 as turning point, 175–77; transfer of patronage to, 160–61; voter shifts of 1930s, 162–64; voter shifts, recent years, 177–78
nativism, 36, 113–15, 124
New Deal, 101, 153, 157, 159, 160–62
New York City, 26, 45, 71, 76, 87, 142; Civil War draft riots, 28, 45–46; ethnic groups, 148; Irish in, 8, 41, 45, 46, 63, 103, Irish in control of, 65–68, 87, 88, 89, 93, 146; Irish leadership loss, 148–49; population figures, 36, 42, 63; St. Patrick's Day Parade, 25, 41; Triangle Shirtwaist fire, 99–101, 123, 136, 187; vote fraud, 80; voting patterns, 161–62; see also Tammany Hall
New York Sun, 8
New York Times, The, 92, 99
Nixon, Richard M., 174–75, 187
"No Irish Need Apply" signs, 41–42, 138
Normans, 10, 15, 16–17, 19
Norris, Frank, 95, 130

O'Banion, Dion (Little Diony), 4, 91
O'Brien, Lawrence, 173

Index

O'Casey, Sean, 4
O'Connell, "Uncle Dan," 88, 171
O'Connor, Edwin, 62
Octopus, The (Norris), 95
O'Donnell, Kenneth, 173
O'Donnell, Myles and Klondike, 91
O'Donnell, Rory, 20
O'Higgins, Bernardo, 19, 188
O'Malley, Frank Ward, 8
O'Neill, Eugene, 107, 130
O'Neill, Hugh, Earl of Tyrone, 17, 20
O'Neill, Thomas P. "Tip," 90, 172
oral history, 10, 15
Ossian, 4
ostracism, 18, 48
Outlook, The, Addams, article, 191–98
Owen, Robert L., 141

PACs (political action committees), 179
"Paddy wagons," 29
Papist Plot theory, 6–7, 27
Parnell, Thomas, 21
parties, political, 11, 95; of 1850s, 36;
   post-Civil War, 51–54, 93–95
patronage, political, 60–62, 68–69, 77–
   80, 89, 185; Roosevelt, 152–53, 160–
   61; Tammany Hall, 87
Pembroke, Earl of, see Strongbow
Pendergast, James, 75, 92
Pendergast, Thomas J., 75, 83–84, 92,
   149, 151, 160, 171
Peoria, Illinois, 64, 88, 93
Perkins, Frances, 101, 106
Philadelphia, 28, 42, 93, 142, 183
Pierce, Franklin, 36
Pittsburgh, 93, 129, 160–61
Plunkitt, George Washington, 67–68, 70–
   71, 77, 82–83, 123, 147, 183
police departments: growth of, 28, 95;
   Irish control of, 7, 28, 29, 50, 59, 65,
   76–77, 89, 104, 129, 130, 149
Polish-Americans, 63, 68, 80, 91, 92, 103,
   148
Polish immigrants, 30, 31, 68
Polk, James K., 35
Powers, David, 173
Powers, Johnny, 68–70, 191
pragmatism, 131, 159, 186; Irish, 12, 31
presidency, U.S., 9, 11, 90, 102, 157;
   issue of religion, 138–41, 174; politics
   of, 106, 111–19, 138–42, 145, 175–
   77; Republican dominance, 52–53, 93–
   95, 111, 131, 141–42, 145;
   Southerners and, 106, 116–19, 175–
   77; see also elections, presidential

Progressive movement, 95, 112, 129
Prohibition, 5, 91, 106, 112, 113–15,
   118, 123, 127, 137, 141, 171
Protestants, 112–13; anti-Catholic bigotry
   in U.S., 27, 40, 89, 113–14, 138–41; in
   Northern Ireland, 20–22
pub, local, role in Irish community life,
   47, 49, 75
public works, 53, 61, 96; graft, 66, 77,
   83; Depression, 150

racism, 46, 52, 53, 114, 124, 176
Radical Republicans, 94
Raskob, John J., 140
recessions (panics), 96
Red Scare of 1920s, 105
Reedy, George (father), 3–6
Reedy family ancestry, 9–10
reformers, 62, 66, 69–70, 79, 81, 101–3,
   130, 171, 184, 186, 187, 196–98
religion, as issue in presidential elections,
   138–41, 174
religious strife, Ireland, 21–22
Republican Party, 93, 94–95, 111, 131;
   and black vote, 177–78; founding of,
   36, 52; labor vote, 162–63; as party of
   business, 52–53, 54, 94, 130, 163;
   presidential politics, 52–53, 94, 111,
   112, 141–42, 145–46; small-town and
   rural voter base of, 52–53, 54, 138,
   162, 178
Reuther, Walter, 82
Roach Guards, 45
Roosevelt, Eleanor, 147
Roosevelt, Franklin D., 19, 83–84, 91,
   100, 101, 106, 111, 118, 146, 147; as
   governor, 142, 145, 152; 1932
   candidacy of, 151–53, 163, 175–76; as
   president, 150, 153, 157, 158–60, 162,
   163–64, 176, 187
Roosevelt, James, 152
Roosevelt, Theodore, 158, 187
Root, Elihu, 101
Rose, Alex, 82, 162
Russell, Sean, 4
Russian Jewish immigrants, 30, 31, 68

Sabath, Adolph J., 148
St. Louis, 89
Saint Patrick, 15–16
St. Patrick's Day, 5, 8, 25, 41
Saltonstall, Leverett, 166, 167
San Francisco, 64, 75, 93, 129
Saxons, 10

Index

Schlesinger, Arthur, 173
Scots: in Northern Ireland, 20–21; in U.S., 12, 28
seanachies (bards), 10, 15
Senate, U.S., 11, 102, 151, 165–67, 188; Irish-Americans in, 107
sexual mores, 48, 125, 183
Seymour, Horatio, 67, 93
"shamus," 29
Shannon, William V., 26, 103
Shaw, George Bernard, 9
Sheehan, William F., 93
Sinclair, Upton, 130
slavery, 11, 36, 38, 52
slums, 39, 40–41, 65, 82
Smith, Alfred E., 76, 83, 100–2, 107, 116–18, 123, 127, 135–37, 151–52, 158, 162, 173, 183, 187; governor, 102, 105–6, 136; 1928 presidential candidacy of, 135–42, 149, 174
Smith, Jim, 102
social change: disinterest of machine politicians in, 62, 69; reform politicians and, 100–3, 105, 136; role of cities in, 39–40, 124
Socialist Party, 105, 115, 149, 163
social services, void filled by Irish machines, 60, 63, 67, 78, 95–96, 184, 192–96
Sorel, Georges, 64
South: and Democratic presidential nominees, 106, 116–19, 175–77; racism, 52, 53, 114, 124, 176; Solid, 94
Southern European immigrants, 30, 31, 68, 80, 113, 115, 184
Spartan Association, 26
state politics, 53, 54, 94, 136; Democratic strength in, 111, 142, 145, 178; entry of Irish into, 101–2, 105–6, 136–37; Tweed and, 66
steel industry, 28, 162–63
Stevenson, Adlai E., 187
Stewart, Charles, 21
stock market crash of 1929, 149–50
strong-arm tactics, 92, 149
Strongbow (Earl of Pembroke), 15, 16–17, 107
Studs Lonigan (Farrell), 146
Sullivan, John L. (Boston Strong Boy), 7, 104
Sullivan, Roger, 90, 102
Sunday, Billy, 113
Sweeney, Peter B. "Brains," 65, 88
Swift, Jonathan, 4
Synge, John Millington, 9, 123

Taggart, Tom, 102
Tammany Hall, 26, 63, 65–68, 70–71, 77, 82, 87–88, 116, 127, 146, 148, 152, 157, 164, 183; beginnings of, 87; reform wing, 101, 118, 135–36
teaching, Irish in, 89
tenant-farmers, Ireland, 20–22
Thomas, Norman, 149
Thompson, William Hale "Big Bill," 81, 91, 127–29
Tilden, Samuel J., 93
Tone, Wolfe, 4, 21
Triangle Shirtwaist fire, 99–101, 105, 123, 136, 187
Truman, Harry, 75, 162, 164, 166, 175
Tuatha Ta Danaan, 15, 19
Tugwell, Rexford, 159
Tumulty, Joseph, 102
Tweed, William Marcy "Boss," 47, 65–66, 67, 76, 83, 84, 88, 123, 149
Tweed Ring, 67, 87–88, 183
Tyrone, County, 20

Ulster, Ireland, 64, 171–72
"Ulster plantation" project, 20–21
underground tactics, Irish, 18, 22, 28
Underwood, Oscar, 118
unions, 64, 65, 77, 81–82, 162–64
United Automobile Workers, 82, 164
United Electrical Workers, 164
United Mine Workers, 162
United Steel Workers, 163, 164
urbanization, 28–29, 32, 36–37, 42, 54, 111, 124, 127; *see also* cities

Valera, Eamon de, 103
verbal transaction in politics, 49–50, 76
Vikings, 10, 16, 19
vote buying, 50–51, 61–62, 77–80, 94, 105, 193, 197
vote fraud, 63, 80–81, 84, 92

Wagner, Robert F., 101, 136, 164
Walker, Jimmy, 71
Walker, Mickey, 9
Walsh, David I., 90, 107, 118, 123, 152
Walsh, Mike, 26
Walsh, Tom, 107
ward leaders, 61, 75–78, 158, 178
WASPs (white Anglo-Saxon Protestants), 7, 11–12, 27, 30, 31, 45, 103, 104, 107, 113, 115, 142
wealth, redistribution of, 31, 63, 67, 196
Webster, Daniel, 35
Western Federation of Miners, 64, 94

[211]

Index

Wheeler, Burton K., 112
Whigs, 36
WHYOs (gangsters), 46–47, 140
Willebrandt, Mabel Walker, 141
Wilson, Woodrow, 53, 94, 101, 102–3, 104, 116, 141, 158, 171, 173, 175
Wobblies (IWW), 64, 94
Wood, Fernando, 65

Woodham-Smith, Cecil, 26
World War I, 103–5, 112–13, 125
World War II, 104, 158
WPA (Works Progress Administration), 160, 161

Yeats, William Butler, 4, 9, 123

George E. Reedy was Lyndon Johnson's press secretary and is now the Nieman Professor of Journalism at Marquette University. He is also the author of *Who Will Do Our Fighting for Us?*, *The Twilight of the Presidency*, *The Presidency in Flux*, *Lyndon B. Johnson: A Memoir*, *The U.S. Senate: Paralysis or Search for Consensus?*, and *The Twilight of the Presidency: Johnson to Reagan*. He lives in Milwaukee, Wisconsin.